Frank sinatra

1915–1998

a tribute

stan britt

Acknowledgements

In such a venture as FRANK SINATRA: A TRIBUTE, the author's own endeavours can
be rendered next-to-useless without the invaluable assistance of any number of
helpers. The following list comprises a group of people whose eagerness to assist
with all manner of inquiries – often made at the most inconvenient times – was
matched only by their desire to produce accuracy, full detail and as speedy a
delivery as possible. If my sometimes fading memory has omitted deserving names,
I can only trust that they will not be offended and they themselves will know that
their noble efforts will have contributed to the book's overall compilation and
factual accuracy.

George Adey, Ken Barnes, Dale Belcher, Colin Britt, Robin Britt, Doreen Browne,
Sammy Cahn, Trisha Coogan (Sony/UK), Don Costa, Fred Dellar, Robert Farnon,
Alan A Freeman, Allan Garrick, Dave Gelly, Dorothy Gosling, Chris Howes, Jo
Kennedy (BMG/UK), Billy May, Loonis McGlohon, Rod McKuen, Brian O'Connor,
Henry Pleasants, Jo Pratt (EMI Records/UK), Ray Purslow (Record Centre,
Birmingham), Tony Radcliffe, Nelson Riddle, J Billy Verplanck, Fred Wadsworth

I WOULD also be lacking in common courtesy should I fail to express my deep
gratitude to my new-found friends at Carlton Books, London. To Sharon Hutton,
for assembling the range of marvellous photos to be found throughout the book.
To Fiona Knowles, for a superbly creative layout-and-design job and to Sarah Larter
and Julian Flanders. In every way, they've been a Top Team!

To: MEB
Without whose inspiration, especially during what will
remain my own Golden Years, this book – like life itself –
would have been absolutely impossible …

Frank sinatra

1915–1998

a tribute

CARLTON

contents

Overture

What this book actually celebrates is the undeniable fact that, for close on six decades, one of the all-time great singing talents was such a compelling factor in the lives of so many people.

As we look back on Sinatra's life, this book endeavours to put into perspective just what an awesome contribution this native North-American-of-Sicilian-extraction made to the world of entertainment.

And if the emphasis here falls principally on Sinatra's personal achievements in raising pop vocalism to an art form, then that's nothing to apologize for. Few if any artists were as productive over as many years. The one regret is that these pages can cover only a tiny number of the 1001 events that made up such a lengthy and industrious career.

Frank Sinatra: A Tribute traces the boyhood days in Hoboken, New Jersey, through the myriad of often complex, occasionally tortuous and always intriguing stories that culminated in Sinatra being crowned the King of Show Business.

But this book doesn't claim to be a blow-by-blow account of Sinatra's action-packed personal life. Far too much literature has been published in previous years relating to Sinatra's private affairs. Whether true or false, much too much of it has been sensational, revealing little about the man's professional talents, let alone what really made him run.

And, throughout all the highs and lows, one thing is certain: Sinatra proved himself the supreme individualist, willing to take risks. All the while, he did it *his* way…

Of course, there were times when Sinatra was less than gracious to many people … frequently towards the press, sometimes even to friends. A hugely-inflated ego complemented by a temper of legendary violence often combined with circumstance to get him into deep trouble. He had his fair share of fights – both verbal and physical – and sometimes in public. A reckless attitude occasionally resulted in disaster.

In Sinatra's defence, he on occasion openly confessed to his failings. And conversely, he always gave generously to charity.

In any case, even if many of the "bad" stories about Sinatra are true, they are of minimal interest to this author. Let others write those …

Occasional references *are* made here to Sinatra's alleged involvement with the underworld, or his attempts to seek gaming licences in the lucrative pastures of Las Vegas. But even these somehow correlate to what this book is all about: the man and his music.

As one of the greatest ever vocalists, Sinatra's contributions may never be surpassed. As a genuinely gifted actor, he made a substantial contribution to Hollywood – winning one Oscar for his acting and receiving another Academy Award nomination. But his acting skills only rarely approached his genius as a singer, especially in concert and as a recording artist.

Light and shade – Sinatra's was a life of celebrity and of achievement.

This book, then, is for those who were touched, deeply or just casually, by his talents – primarily by his unique qualities as a singer. For, above all, he remains the Poet Laureate of the Popular Song.

Sinatra
the Voice
of Popular
Music

Even before he came into his own as a performer, Frank

Sinatra always sounded like Frank Sinatra and nobody else.

Originally, though, it was Bing Crosby who triggered off

Sinatra's unstoppable quest to become the very best singer

around. Following a trip to Jersey City to see the incomparable

crooner in concert, Sinatra discovered his destiny.

Impressed by Crosby's persuasive way with a song, Sinatra vowed that his own approach to singing would be equally individualistic. He would be beholden to no other performer for his style, not even the all-powerful, much-imitated Crosby.

It is worth remembering that until the emergence of Sinatra at the end of the Thirties, Crosby had been the reigning King of Pop Vocalism and, together with Louis Armstrong, Billie Holiday and Al Jolson, one of the great innovators of his craft.

Bing could swing with the best of them but his real magic was reserved for ballads. As his voice deepened with the years, developing real warmth and tonal quality, he became the first pop-vocal superstar of the Thirties and reigned as undisputed King until Sinatra's arrival on the scene ...

But, although Crosby's ability to project songs made a profound impression, this was not the way Frank Sinatra wanted to sing. Even at an early stage, Sinatra had strong views about not becoming just another Crosby clone – he would attempt a completely different approach.

As he told *Life International* magazine, some 30 years after that milestone Crosby concert, "I decided to experiment a little and come up with something different. What I finally hit upon was more the *bel canto* Italian school of singing, without making a point of it. That meant I had to stay in better shape because I had to sing more. It was more difficult than Crosby's style, much more difficult."

The style he came up with has indeed been compared to the Italian *bel canto* ("beautiful singing") form of operatic singing, characterized by its rich tonal lyricism and a bravura display of vocal technique.

Henry Pleasants, the noted vocal music expert, detects *bel canto* influence in Sinatra's work. In a personal interview with the author during the late Seventies, he cited Sinatra's "absolute mastery of the use of *appoggiatura* – when a singer inserts an extra note between two other notes, thus giving expressive emphasis, and elegance to a cadence. Just as important, he was always aware of when best to use it ... and when not to."

Crosby provided the trigger for Sinatra's career in showbusiness.

Without doubt, Sinatra's seamless phrasing was, as Pleasants insists, uncannily close to the Italian vocal school. However, there were two important ingredients of Sinatra's style that are not considered obligatory in *bel canto*. Firstly, his insistence on setting emotion above mere technique; and, secondly, his joyous brand of musical humour – something for which *bel canto* singing is hardly renowned.

In fact, Sinatra went to great lengths to build up his "effortless" brand of singing. In the same *Life International* interview, he recalled how deeply affected he was by the *legato* ballad playing of his former boss, orchestra leader Tommy Dorsey. "He would take a musical phrase and play it all the way through seemingly without breathing, for 8, 10 or maybe 16 bars."

Close scrutiny during the two-and-a-half years he spent with the famous trombonist's band – constantly trying to figure out how Dorsey breathed through a held note – convinced Sinatra that this was the kind of phrasing he needed for his own singing style. To achieve extra lung-power, he swam regularly, including much time spent holding his breath under water, and worked out frequently at a local running track.

From the outset, Frank Sinatra's approach to singing was supremely conversational. Without neglecting the melodic line or the need to imbue a performance with rhythm and swing, the words were of top concern at all times.

Mabel Mercer – her impeccable diction had a profound influence on Sinatra's style.

To this end, Sinatra perfected his own special kind of diction. Consonants, rather than vowels, were always stressed. But however individual his singing became, his influences should not be forgotten. Crosby of course provided the springboard for his aspirations but it was from Mabel Mercer that Sinatra learned about diction. Through years of performing in small, intimate New York clubs, Mabel Mercer had established a near-legendary reputation for putting across lyrics with conviction.

Pianist-composer Loonis McGlohon has made a living out of providing sensitive, eloquent accompaniments for top-class singers.

"I learned about leaving breathing space for singers by listening to singers breathe. Particularly Mabel Mercer. You've got to wait to hear where they breathe. Sometimes they'd put a comma in a different place ... Mabel and Frank – I have to lock them together in this instance – would always do the proper punctuation in a song. And I'm sure Frank learned a lot about this from Mabel."

However much he learned from Crosby and Mercer, Sinatra's biggest debt was owed to Billie Holiday. He was deeply affected by her innate sense of timing and the heart-on-sleeve approach she took to singing, especially the kind of sad ballads that he would make his own as the years unfolded. Billie sang about life in the raw, with a couldn't-give-a-damn style that must have appealed to Frank's own brand of arrogance – and his own intuitive appreciation of lyric interpretation.

Sinatra found Holiday a kindred spirit in other basic ways. For, as his own talent began to unfold, the sexual content in his delivery grew stronger and more obvious to rivals hers. Like Billie Holiday too, Sinatra often operated on a short fuse. This, together with his own Sicilian background, no doubt gave his singing added bite and, from the Fifties on, a visceral edge that communicated itself to audiences.

Sinatra openly acknowledged his debt to Lady Day. During an interview with *Ebony* magazine in 1958, he declared,

"With few exceptions, every major pop singer in the United States during her generation has been touched in some way by her genius. It is Billie Holiday, whom I first heard in 52nd Street clubs in the early-Thirties, who was, and still remains, the greatest single musical influence on me."

Early on, as a singer with Harry James and Tommy Dorsey, Sinatra's ambitions were held in check by a fairly rigid stylistic format that allowed little scope for self-expression. Numbers were confined for the most part to what dance band musicians once called jig tempo – a basic medium-paced, restrained swing.

"All Or Nothing At All" remains the best-known of the nine items Sinatra recorded with James. And even though he had not yet developed into a true lyric interpreter, there was no doubting the unrestrained passion of his delivery, or the obvious sincerity in his reading of the words.

With both James and Dorsey, Sinatra's speciality was always as a ballad singer. From a rhythmic standpoint, he showed little outstanding ability initially, although he handled himself adequately in this area.

Sinatra may have been an incomplete swinger at this stage but his singing on songs like "East Of The Sun" (arranged by Sy Oliver) and "Head On My Pillow" (with a chart by Axel Stordahl) does not embarrass him. Wisely, he chose to relax and allow the fine rhythmic impulses radiated by drummer Buddy Rich, pianist Joe Bushkin and the rest of the rhythm section to do the rest.

By the mid-Forties, Sinatra was well on his way to fusing all the elements into a totally individual vocal style. It remains something of an unexplained mystery to this writer that there are certain long-time Sinatra admirers who tend to gloss over his singing during the Forties. In terms of pure vocal quality, his work from this time has rarely been surpassed.

True, the voice sometimes lacked the full-bodied quality that was to come; the extra depth of expression and know-how that would illuminate his singing from the Fifties onwards was not readily apparent in the Forties. And an ability to produce satisfying rhythm performances was something of a rarity. But when it came to ballads, with his right-hand man arranger Axel Stordahl in almost uncanny rapport, Sinatra could do little wrong.

One of the encouraging aspects of his recordings during this halcyon period was that he not only recorded the new pops of the day – including those emanating from Broadway and Hollywood – but he also breathed new life into oldies such as "Embraceable You", "Someone To Watch Over Me", "You Go To My

Happy reunion. Sinatra swings again with Harry James – live, in Los Angeles, 1979.

Head", "These Foolish Things" and "She's Funny That Way". And the boundless confidence of the man enabled him to embrace more ambitious works such as "Bess, Oh Where's My Bess?" (from *Porgy & Bess*), "Ol' Man River" (*Showboat*) and the extended "Soliloquy" from *Carousel*.

Whatever you think of Sinatra, one thing is absolutely certain: he was the single greatest live performer, ever. The greatest live performer, let us be clear, not the greatest live entertainer.

Not that Sinatra did not entertain – far from it. But he didn't play piano or a guitar or any kind of musical instrument. Nor did he dance, juggle or perform magical tricks. He had had a fairly snappy line in comedy at his concerts for decades but this was a regular part of his concert programme, principally to allow him to catch his breath along the way and to introduce his accompanists.

No, Frank Sinatra just sang. And, therefore, he was able to totally commit his talents to doing just that one thing.

Scarcely a dynamic personality in his early days, it's perhaps odd that at that time Sinatra had such an extraordinary ability to communicate with his audiences. It was more than just his singing voice. To many, he may have been an unimposing figure – a skinny young man whose on-stage persona was that of a somewhat fragile, unassertive guy clinging to a stand-up mike ... who just sang.

Yet it was that quality of vulnerability which created immediate rapport with his audience during the band-singing years – an audience which was comprised mostly, though not exclusively, of young women. Part of that appeal could be explained by his country's involvement in World War II and the relative absence of young men. But there was more to the Sinatra phenomenon.

In some media quarters, it used to be obligatory to review Sinatra's appearances in terms of his lack of *avoirdupois*, to criticize the way he dressed and, of course, the near-hysterical reactions of his bobbysox-clad fans. Only the more discerning newspaper critics and the quality jazz magazines bothered to mention his vocal technique or his distinctive approach on stage.

Taking it easy – Sinatra relaxes backstage before a gig, and in the recording studio.

Even after he'd decided on a solo career, the critics clung to their view of this shy little guy and the silly little teenagers who'd one day grow up and forget about their Frankie. Those kind of critics would have been shocked by the suggestion that part of Sinatra's appeal lay in the sexual content of his work.

After his Oscar-winning role in *From Here To Eternity* came a remarkable professional metamorphosis – he began to be taken seriously. Although the brash, hard-drinking, arrogant personality that now emerged was, we are told, already well-known to friends and colleagues, the kind of visceral, hard-swinging singer that emerged as the "new" Sinatra produced a *volte-face* among critics, who had so often put the boot in before.

Suddenly, Sinatra was "The Man". And, critics queued up to have their names put on the door at venues where he was appearing. It is common knowledge that Sinatra himself was hip to this sudden reappraisal: he never forgave those who'd put him down – especially during the dark days.

But Sinatra rarely disappointed those who came to his gigs. On stage, his deportment was impeccable. Even just the way he'd walk from one side of a stage to the other was an event. His occasional use of a small handful of props – like the combination of a stool, a lighted cigarette and a glass of some undetermined liquid – enabled him with great subtlety and effectiveness to create a bar-room scene, or enhance what were invariably definitive readings of classic saloon songs like "Angel Eyes" or "One For My Baby".

One of Sinatra's most significant on-stage gifts was his unparalleled use of the hand microphone. During his earliest days, Sinatra had realized the potential for relaying even the most *sotto voce* phrase by sophisticated use of the microphone. In those days, vocalists perforce used microphones of the strictly stand-up variety – usually square-shaped and attached to a length of piping and a base.

During his *Life International* interview in 1965, Sinatra emphasized how "tremendously important" the use of a microphone was. Many singers, he said, never learned. "They never understood, and still don't, that a microphone is their instrument. It's like they are part of an orchestra, but instead of playing a saxophone they're playing a microphone."

And his perfectionist approach to this aspect of live performance stretched to using a black microphone, "so that it will melt into my dinner jacket and the audience isn't aware of it ... " Sinatra's interest in what could be done with this "instrument" had begun on the fateful occasion when he first went to see Crosby in concert: we don't know how Crosby used his microphone in Jersey

City, but it was impressive enough to exercise a profound influence over Frank's career.

Sinatra, out of retirement in the Seventies, sings again, in Paris.

Even in his "shy guy" days, Frank Sinatra always exuded a kind of charisma. But from the Fifties and thereafter his charisma became a significant element in concert. Whether on stage at the Sands or Caesar's Palace – his two most frequent ports of call on the Las Vegas circuit – or at Carnegie Hall or the Royal Festival Hall, wherever he went, he generated the kind of electricity that few others could match. Even before he made his entry, the air was often charged with excitement. And if he was feeling good, the voice was in tip-top shape and the audience was responsive, there would be a quality that is best described as "magic".

Little wonder, then, that it's so often been said that there was no other place on earth where Frank Sinatra found more happiness and fulfilment than performing on stage before a large audience, and with a large orchestra behind him.

Sinatra's own philosophy about performing was summarized in a comment he made years ago: "If you want to get an audience with you, there's only one way. You have to reach out to them with total honesty and humility. You can be the most artistically perfect performer in the world, but an audience is like a broad – if you're indifferent, endsville!"

Rarely did the musicians who worked alongside Sinatra have anything but praise for the way he went about his job. Indeed, long

ago he set the standard for live performance by not only insisting on his own key musicians, but also by naming and fully crediting the composers and arrangers of each song on stage. And though he may have been critical of mistakes by others, he was always generous with his praise.

Talk with singers, musicians, songwriters or arrangers and you'll find that each one has a particular reason for admiring Sinatra's singing. Although most musical persons enjoy his rhythmic work, by far the largest majority state a marked preference for his way with a ballad. In this context, it's his matchless skills at musical storytelling which come out on top.

It was *Songs For Young Lovers* – Sinatra's first micro-groove LP and his first album for Capitol – that showed he was eminently capable of producing superb, loosely swinging work to put him on a par with practically any of his contemporaries. But it was *Songs For Swingin' Lovers* that ultimately turned out to be his most popular album from any period and which enabled Sinatra to prove his rhythmic point in the company of his most famous musical associate, Nelson Riddle. The combination produced some of the most glorious recorded vocal-instrumental music ever produced.

By the time he laid down those tracks, Sinatra had come up with a highly personal, dynamic method of swinging. It wasn't totally jazz – but it certainly swung! Indeed, there were occasions when he produced swing-singing as good as the best out-and-out jazz vocalists – occasionally, even better.

Writer-broadcaster Dave Gelly once described Sinatra's approach to swing as being "a very businesslike thing". At the same time, he compared it to the no-nonsense, straight-ahead jazz players like Harry Edison, Ben Webster and Zoot Sims. "It's that sort of unfussy singing – there's very little in the way of decoration. It's all down to a precise placement of notes in relation to rhythm, so that you get a song to swing.

"The magical way that Sinatra does this involves both the precise placement of notes and an ability to reflect the conversational nature of the song. This is his thing, and something which he shares with a very short list of other singers, a highly-distinguished group of whom the supreme example is Billie ... When you see him in person, and he's singing songs which swing, the sort of note placement that Miles Davis has, is what he's got."

Ultimately though, in any serious reassessment of Sinatra, it comes down to the ballads to provide the final definition of his art. From the Fifties, one can cite, not just individual tracks, but whole LPs: *In The Wee Small Hours*; *Close To You*; *Where Are You?*; *No One Cares*; and above all the extraordinary, gut-level *Only the Lonely*.

In subsequent years, Sinatra's recordings – like his concert repertoire – provided fascinating examples of his musical flexibility. Not all of them proved a complete success. But Sinatra never was afraid to make the occasional error of judgement – indeed at times he seems to have positively courted disaster.

At least, though, he didn't lack the guts to try something new. By the time he reached his eightieth year, it became apparent that we were not going to be see anymore of Frank Sinatra the concert artist. It is all too easy to trot out the cliché-of-clichés: we shall never see or hear another Frank Sinatra in our lifetimes. But it is true. Certainly, we now have to judge him as a vocalist of unmatched achievements, someone who elevated himself into the area of total respect reserved for the great classical or opera performers of this century.

It is true also because the set of circumstances which came together long ago in a New Jersey port will never occur again. For better or worse, the action-packed life and times of Francis Albert Sinatra can never be repeated. Perhaps the best summation was made many years ago, by another truly great singer of the twentieth-century, and the person who triggered off his burning zeal to become the greatest in his field, Bing Crosby.

"Frank Sinatra is the kind of singer who comes along once in a lifetime – but why did it have to be my lifetime?"

The Embryonic Sinatra

Francis Albert Sinatra was born in Hoboken, New Jersey, on December 12, 1915, the only child of immigrants Martin and Nathalie ("Dolly") Sinatra.

One way or another, Frank Sinatra has achieved a lasting reputation as a fighter. This started the day he was born, weighing in at an impressive 13-and-a-half pounds. Being so large, his birth was difficult and forceps had to be used for the delivery, resulting in permanent scarring on the left side of Sinatra's head.

Much more alarming, though, was the fact that Baby Sinatra hadn't uttered a sound; nor indeed did he appear to be breathing. With enviable presence of mind, Rosa Garavente, Dolly Sinatra's mother, lifted an apparently lifeless infant body, then ran cold water over it. At once, the Sinatra vocal cords sprang into action for the first time.

Young Francis Albert poses with Mama – and not a smile in sight.

Hoboken was a tough place to grow up. With its labyrinth of railway marshalling yards and factory buildings, it was a dreary, grimy port, not far from Jersey City but separated from the bright lights of New York City and Manhattan by the wide Hudson River. For most of his working life, Martin Sinatra was employed at the Hoboken Fire Department. In his spare time, he was also a prize-fighter – under the name of "Marty O'Brien". Dolly Sinatra exercised strict control over young Frank, who tended to be something of a loner. From an early age, he learnt to stand up for himself.

By all accounts, Sinatra was a modest pupil at the David E. Rue Junior High School, from which he graduated in January, 1931. Later the same year, he dropped out of the A. J. Demarest High School (in his sophomore year). And, apart from a short period spent at the Drake Business School, that was where his formal education ended.

Career wise, Sinatra wasn't sure what to do. He was briefly employed on the staff of the local *Jersey Observer* as a truck loader and copy-boy. He also worked as an apprentice ship's riveter. In fact, the youthful Sinatra's mind was on other things. He loved the cinema and music had begun to exert an ever-increasing influence on his thinking. The acquisition of a ukulele, given him when he was 15 by an uncle, provided the incentive to try his hand at singing. Sinatra used to accompany himself as he attempted to reproduce the songs he was hearing day by day on

the wireless – from the likes of Gene Austin, Rudy Vallee, Russ Columbo and, above all, Bing Crosby.

Francis A. Sinatra with Demarest High's glee club.

Indeed, it was after Sinatra had taken regular girlfriend Nancy Barbato to see Crosby live at Loew's Theater in Jersey City in March 1934, that the die was finally cast. Watching Crosby perform, Sinatra became convinced that he too had the kind of talent to make it to the top.

However, it took six years of hard work before Frank Sinatra gained his first real toe-hold on the ladder to success.

To get started, Sinatra had to take his courage in both hands and present himself on stage at numerous amateur or semi-professional talent contests. These took place in a variety of venues, often in noisy roadhouses and social clubs, and most of the time Sinatra was performing for nothing more than a bite to eat.

During these formative years, Sinatra single mindedly sought out as much exposure as possible. He even did *unpaid* live appearances, anything that would bring his name and voice before a wider audience.

A major stepping stone was his appearance on a popular, long-running radio show called *Major Bowes And His Original Amateur Hour*. Broadcast by NBC, the show was an open invitation to possible fame and fortune for hundreds of aspiring performers.

Sinatra auditioned for the contest at New York's Capitol Theater and passed with ease. Major Bowes suggested he join forces with a vocal trio from Hoboken, known as the Three Flashes. Soon the Three Flashes died and the Hoboken Four were born in their stead.

**"Frank Sinatra Day",
October 10, 1947: Fire
Captain Martin Sinatra
crowns his son's day.**

The new group – with Frank singing lead – appeared at the next *Amateur Hour* event on September 8, 1935. They sang the Mack/Brown/Dabney original "Shine", immortalized by Louis Armstrong, and won the contest hands down. Their victory was the biggest in the history of the competition and the Hoboken Four joined Bowes' regular travelling troupe.

Sinatra's membership of the Hoboken Four only lasted for a couple of months, the time it took the group to reach the West Coast. By then, the lead vocalist was bored with the routine of touring. One report has suggested matters came to a head after a heated dispute between Sinatra and the others: they were beginning to resent his growing popularity – he was just getting to like it.

In the end, Sinatra left abruptly for home. Reunited with family and friends, he was ready to make a second attempt at a career in singing – this time as a *solo* singer.

Despite disapproving of her son's ambitions, Dolly Sinatra gave Frank $65 to purchase his own portable public-address system. Always forward thinking, Sinatra added his own personal library of printed orchestrations – "stocks" – for use by any of the accompanying bands with which he found employment.

For a while, Sinatra held down a regular job at the Union, a Hoboken social club, earning $40 a week. This ended after Sinatra failed to persuade the management to install facilities that would allow him to broadcast from the premises. He had more success persuading the bosses of several stations in the New York and New Jersey areas to allow him to perform on radio ... for nothing.

His next two moves were of real significance. First, he landed a regular job at the Rustic Cabin, a popular roadhouse not too far from Alpine, New Jersey. Even at the audition, he was quick to note that the Rustic Cabin had facilities for broadcasting. Then, on February 4, 1939, Sinatra wed Nancy Barbato at Our Lady of Sorrows Catholic Church, Jersey City.

At the Cabin, Sinatra was kept busy for his $15-a-week-plus-tips. He sang solo, of course, with the resident Harold Arden Orchestra. But he also acted as master of ceremonies and showed customers to their tables.

Towards the end of the 18-month residency, one of Sinatra's local broadcasts paid off handsomely. His singing was heard on the radio one evening by a tall, whippet-thin trumpet player/band leader, who was listening in on his hotel radio. After establishing an international reputation with Benny Goodman, Harry James had recently put together his own big-band.

At this time, James badly needed a good, reliable boy singer, and so he decided on a visit to the Rustic Cabin, together with his manager. Both were highly impressed. Right away, they asked Sinatra if he would join the Harry James Orchestra. Salary: $75 a week. Almost immediately, a two-year contract was drawn up and signed ... and the roadhouse lost its personable, super-confident young singer. Sinatra raced home to break the news to Nancy at their three-room apartment home in Jersey City. Now, he told her, the days of hustling radio stations were over. And there would be no more waiter jobs.

The gig with James was just the kind of break Frank had been working his butt off to get. And, no doubt, he told Nancy,

"This is just the first step, honey. Now, I'm on my way ... "

R E T R O S P E C T I V E S
1935-1939

GIGS

Very little material has surfaced which gives more than an inkling of the kind of singing voice Sinatra possessed before he joined the Harry James Orchestra. Indeed, there are just two examples of his work with the Hoboken Four. Both emanate from appearances on the *Amateur Hour* shows.

The first – and best-known – is "Shine", recorded at New York's Capitol Theater on September 8, 1935. After Sinatra had self-consciously introduced the group, the Hoboken Four produced an up-tempo, somewhat dated version of the jazz-based standard. The performance gives little indication of greater things to come. The same can be said of the treatment they meted out to "The Curse Of An Aching Heart", broadcast some time later in 1935.

Both numbers, however, are now of enormous historical interest and available on albums such as the British-made CD, *The Frank Sinatra Story/Forty Swing & Ballad Classics from '39–53*.

More revealing, perhaps – and contained within the same CD release – is "Our Love", co-written by Larry Clinton, Buddy Bernier and Bob Emmerich and freely adapted from Tchaikovsky's *Romeo And Juliet*. This was recorded privately by Sinatra as a demo disc with orchestral accompaniment by Frank Manne. There *are* elements of the Sinatra-to-come on this rare disc, which, presumably, he – or Dolly – must have paid for. The production of demo discs by up-and-coming performers was something of a rarity in 1939 – even private demos.

It was a further indication of just how dedicated the young man from Hoboken, NJ, was to getting on in show business …

MOVIES

Sinatra's earliest involvement with motion pictures came from his association with Major Bowes. He took part in two shorts, under the collective heading of *Major Bowes' Amateur Theatre Off The Air*, both were made in 1935 and released through RKO. Young Sinatra played a waiter in the first and then "blacked-up" for a bit part in *The Big Minstrel Act*.

RECORDINGS

Of all the rare early performances that have turned up in recent times, the most bizarre is included on a CD, aptly titled *The Rarest Sinatra*. Taken from a *Town Hall Tonight* show, it features Sinatra conducting (?) the Four Sharps, a less-than-promising Dixieland-jazz outfit. Under Sinatra's supervision, the Sharps go through an awful version of "Exactly Like You".

For more than one obvious reason, this song is just about the rarest of all the rare Sinatra "performances" …!

The Band-Singing Years

ON NUMEROUS occasions over the years, Frank Sinatra was always delighted to reaffirm that the six months he spent with the Harry James Orchestra were among the happiest of all his musical experiences.

For one thing, Sinatra found Harry James to be a friendly and supportive leader. James, a native of Albany, Georgia, knew he'd signed a most promising vocalist and wanted to encourage him as much as possible. There was one sticky moment when James suggested it might, perhaps, be helpful if the singer changed his name. Sinatra was appalled – and adamant. It was the name he'd been born with and it was the name he would continue to use forever – in *every* area of his life. His new boss soon got the message …

Harry Haag James (1916–83) had established an enviable reputation as a superbly-gifted, fiery trumpet soloist with the star-studded Benny Goodman Orchestra. His early background found him helping his father, a bandmaster, in a circus. It was James Sr who gave his son trumpet lessons at the age of 10: the youngster took to the instrument like a duck to water. A full-time career in music beckoned when James joined the Ben Pollack band in 1935 at the age of 19. James' solo work with Pollack soon impressed Goodman and it was in his band that the tall, lean James came of age as a major jazz instrumentalist. By the time that he left to front his own big-band, like fellow stars, Krupa, Hampton and Wilson, James had become one of the top virtuosi of the Swing Era.

With so much competition in the big-band field, success didn't come easy for the Harry James Orchestra, even though James had borrowed $4,500 from Goodman, in return for a one-third interest, and received further financial support from the Willard Alexander Agency. James' first outfit contained precious few outstanding soloists – apart from the leader himself, of

Harry James' warmth of character was such that he did not stand in Sinatra's way when the young singer wanted out.

course. Dave Matthews, a dependable, versatile saxophonist and arranger, was one and Jack Gardner, the band's first piano player, was another. James, the leader, was still not quite sure whether he should concentrate on a mainly jazz-based musical policy, or whether, like others, he should attempt to accommodate non-jazzers, who made up the largest potential audience. With practical considerations in mind, James must have realized the importance of including at least one singer in the band's line-up.

It was Sinatra who became James' first male vocalist, sharing duties with dark-haired, petite Connie Haines, the replacement for Bernice Byers who had left after just a few months. Trumpeter Jack Palmer handled novelty and jazzy offerings.

In the six months he spent with the band, Sinatra learned how to project his singing to different kinds of audiences at a variety of venues. He also took part in radio broadcasts and made his debut proper on record. His wife Nancy was present for his first-ever appearance with the band at the Baltimore Hippodrome during June 1939. The new boy singer sang just two numbers: "My Love For You" and "Wishing (Will Make It So)".

Sinatra's next important appearances with the James band took place at the Roseland Ballroom, New York, during the 1939 World Fair. After one of the gigs, he received his very first notice – Sinatra had pleaded with the band manager to ask journalist George T. Simon to give him a mention. Simon duly obliged. His *Metronome* review spoke of "the very pleasing vocals of Frank Sinatra, whose easy phrasing is especially commendable".

Working with James taught Sinatra about the importance of real camaraderie. There were no clashes of temperament between the sidemen, and everyone – singers and instrumentalists included – respected James, both personally and musically. Never a martinet (unlike Goodman), Harry James led by example, both on- and off-stage. A genuine friendship developed between him and his male singer that would last until the band leader's death some 44 years later.

Happy singin', swingin' days with Dorsey. Frank and the Pied Pipers in sweet harmony. Joe Bushkin's happy, too.

When Sinatra told James he would like to accept an invitation to join the prestigious Tommy Dorsey Orchestra, it was James' warmth of character and keen understanding of the other man's ambition which led him to tear up their two-year contract.

For Dorsey, pursuit of Sinatra was a second attempt to find an adequate replacement for singer Jack Leonard, who had left in November. The "average only" Allan DeWitt had proved a less-than-satisfactory substitute for the long-serving Leonard.

In fact, it was Leonard himself who, having heard Sinatra's "All Or Nothing At All", with James, played the record to Dorsey. Ironically, Sinatra then auditioned for the bespectacled trombonist-leader by singing Irving Berlin's "Marie" … Leonard's most famous feature with Dorsey and one of the band's most popular items.

Sinatra said "Yes" to Dorsey almost before the band leader had popped the vital question.

Tommy Dorsey was impressed enough to offer the job to Sinatra on the spot, along with a weekly salary cheque that was almost twice as much as the $75 James had been paying him.

Sinatra said "Yes" almost before Dorsey had popped the question. The prestige of working with such a well-known band may have been uppermost in his mind, but the increase in salary was more than welcome – especially since Nancy was pregnant.

And then there were three – Frank and Nancy with their first-born, Nancy, Jr.

With Tommy Dorsey, Sinatra's aspirations, which sometimes seemed wild and slightly ridiculous to some of his less ambitious new colleagues, could begin to take root. Musically, too, the Sinatra vocal style was about to receive enormous assistance. The leader's exceptional trombone playing, for instance, was set to influence deeply the way Sinatra controlled his breathing, which in turn would become the basis for the seamless phrasing Sinatra used so effectively on ballads.

Above all, Sinatra admired the sheer professionalism of his sometimes tetchy band leader, as well as his constant quest for musical perfection. Tommy Dorsey demanded the utmost from his men and made sure he got it. Even though singing credits on the first records were limited to the anonymous "With Vocal Refrain" – something which must have miffed Sinatra immensely – the name of the new vocalist soon became well known to collectors of the band's recordings. Indeed, there were times when the leader came to resent the fact that Sinatra seemed to be attracting wilder applause during an evening's performance than either Dorsey himself or the band. The skinny singer held an almost uncanny fascination for the younger female members of the audience.

In the early Forties, the itinerary of a highly successful orchestra like Dorsey's tended to be exhausting, imposing rigorous demands upon musicians. One-nighter followed one-nighter, whether the band was on tour or playing an extended season at one of the plush hotels or night-spots, where the prospect of three or four – sometimes more – shows was the norm.

None of this seemed to worry Frank Sinatra, who was anxious to learn as much as possible about each area of activity in which the Dorsey outfit participated. He was quietly absorbing it all for future reference, and his knowledge of recording techniques expanded rapidly. Indeed, between February 1940 and July 1942, Sinatra appeared on 84 Tommy Dorsey titles, mostly singing solo but sometimes with the assistance of the Pied Pipers, the band's fine vocal quartet, and occasionally in tandem with Connie Haines, his erstwhile colleague with Harry James.

Sinatra's deep interest in studio work no doubt served him well when it came to a most unusual event on January 19, 1942. Although still officially an employee of Tommy Dorsey, Frank participated in his first solo recording date.

The session produced four sides, arranged and conducted by

Axel Stordahl, who had penned many of the singer's charts with the Dorsey band. Released on Bluebird, a subsidiary of Victor – the label for which the Tommy Dorsey Orchestra recorded – the four songs provided Sinatra's boss with advance warning that, sooner or later, he was going to have to look for a replacement boy singer.

And the inclusion of strings, a harp and woodwinds in the fourteen-piece accompanying ensemble showed the future direction, musically speaking, in which Sinatra was headed.

When his number one crowd pleaser finally asked to be released from his contract in order to go solo, Tommy Dorsey turned out to be no Harry James – even though he was given the luxury of a whole year's notice. Sinatra's entreaties eventually won the day, but not before the most detailed financial and legal negotiations had been completed to the satisfaction of all parties.

First, Dorsey offered his departing vocalist $17,000 to sign a contract, which would result in Dorsey's pocketing 33⅓ per cent of Sinatra's gross earnings over $100 for the next 10 years, plus an additional 10 per cent to the band leader's personal manager as a commission for introducing Frank Sinatra to Columbia Records. Sinatra duly signed in August 1942 but that was not the end of the matter.

Dorsey was incensed to read interviews given by Sinatra complaining bitterly at the former's financial stranglehold over him. He sued. It took until the following August for the matter to be resolved. The MCA Agency offered Dorsey $60,000. Dorsey accepted. In addition, MCA paid Dorsey $35,000 to obtain Sinatra as a client, with Sinatra himself coughing up an additional $25,000 – borrowed from Columbia's Manie Sachs – as an advance against future royalties on his Columbia recordings.

And just to top-and-tail what had by now become a real music-biz *cause celebre*, MCA agreed to split its commissions on Sinatra with GAO, with whom he had signed immediately on leaving the Dorsey band. Although Tommy Dorsey expressed satisfaction over the final arrangements, he was not at all pleased with losing not only his principal vocalist but also one of his most gifted arranging talents into the bargain. For Axel Stordahl left with Sinatra, who offered him a monthly salary considerably larger than that paid out by Dorsey ...

Las Vegas Nights: Dorsey, Rich, Elman, Connie Haines and a watchful Sinatra (right)

RECORDS

ALTHOUGH, during the band-singing years, there was only one, rather special, occasion when Frank Sinatra actually recorded under his own name, there were many regular visits to the recording studio – especially when he was working with Tommy Dorsey's Orchestra.

The song "All Or Nothing At All" exemplified Sinatra's commitment to lyrics.

Obviously, in six months' service as Harry James' boy singer, chances to record were limited. And, frankly, the 10 different titles he cut with James, between July and November, 1939, offered but gentle hints of what was to come rather than definitive examples of Sinatra's art. Best of the bunch were "All Or Nothing At All", "It's Funny To Everyone But Me" and "On A Little Street In Singapore" (the last-named song was revived, with success, 39 years later by the superb Manhattan Transfer vocal group).

"All Or Nothing At All" – with its near-falsetto ending – had a chequered history. On its original release, it racked up meagre sales of 8,000. Wisely, Columbia Records re-issued the side four years later when the spotlight was firmly on Sinatra, the solo performer. This time, however, the disc not only became a triumphant chart-topper but it also went on to achieve reported sales of around one million copies.

In a highly-dramatic way, it also indicated the kind of commitment the singer could bring to the lyrics of a song, an ability which was to become more and more striking over the next few years – a technique which would become a vital ingredient of Sinatra's basic approach to his overall vocal concept.

Less dramatic, but containing their own mix of poignancy and vulnerability, were "Singapore" and "It's Funny", which likewise held out promise for the future. The remainder of Sinatra's output with the Harry James band remains primarily of historical importance. None of the other songs Sinatra was called upon to record offered much in the way of inspiration, although the 1922-published "My Buddy" still carries a kind of dated charm. All the titles listed above, including three alternative takes, are contained on the album *Harry James & His Orchestra, Featuring Frank Sinatra: The Complete Recordings 1939.*

Live recordings of Sinatra-James fare remain scarce, although in recent times several interesting airchecks have been made available on LP or CD. Taken from broadcasts dated July and August 1939, the seven Sinatra-James performances contained within *Harry*

James & His Orchestra Featuring Frank Sinatra/ All Or Nothing At All are basically similar to the early commercial recordings in showing Sinatra's singing ability at this early stage.

Perhaps the single most interesting aspect of these rare performances is the fact that not one of the numbers made it into the Columbia recording studios. For some reason, neither Sinatra nor James – together, or apart – ever made commercial recordings of such items as "If I Didn't Care", "Wishing" and "The Lamp Is Low". Once more, though, these excerpts of broadcasts add significantly to our knowledge of the singer's burgeoning career ...

The next stage, featuring Sinatra's considerable output as a member of the Tommy Dorsey Orchestra, still makes for absorbing listening. After six months' apprenticeship with James, this period represented the focal point of Sinatra's band-singing days, a time which saw him graduate into the ranks of polished performers, ready for his solo career.

The first Sinatra-Dorsey sessions, however, showed only a marginal improvement on the recordings with James. For instance, Sinatra's singing at the first date with Tommy Dorsey in February 1940 sounded strained. There was nothing actually wrong with his versions of "The Sky Fell Down" (significantly, arranged by Axel Stordahl) or "Too Romantic" (interestingly, a new Burke-Van Heusen number, featured in *The Road To Singapore*, the latest Bob Hope/Bing Crosby movie). But there was little sign of the deep-felt emotion that was later to become the trademark of Sinatra's singing. Nor were his great abilities as a lyric-interpreter yet in evidence.

Yet Sinatra's keen interest in the art of recording really developed during his first year with Dorsey. Session by session,

there were signs of improving technique. For instance, "I'll Be Seeing You" (from the second session, also in February) had a vocal chorus with a touching quality which few, if any, of Sinatra's band-singing rivals of the period could match. So, too, did "Polka Dots And Moonbeams" – the first Sinatra-Dorsey disc to enter the Hit Parade, albeit for a brief, one-week stay. At an April 23 date, Sinatra sounded more comfortable, accompanied on three of the five mastered titles by the Dorsey Sentimentalists, an eight-piece unit drawn from the full orchestra and featuring all-too-brief muted trumpet from the once-great, now-ailing Bunny Berigan.

The following session remains important, not only because it was the first occasion on which Sinatra recorded as temporary lead with the Pied Pipers, but because the resulting "I'll Never Smile Again" went on to become a smash hit, spending an amazing 12 weeks as the USA's Number 1 record. By the end of the year, Sinatra-featured discs were becoming regular visitors to the Hit Parade. As his personal popularity grew and grew during 1941, the Sinatra-Dorsey hits kept coming. "Oh, Look At Me Now", co-authored by Joe Bushkin, the band's pianist, with Frank joined by Connie Haines and the Pipers, missed the top spot by just one place; however, "Dolores", also cut in January 1941, achieved the feat.

In 1942, Sinatra vocals helped no fewer than 12 releases to reach the charts, with "There Are Such Things" spending six weeks in the Number 1 position. But, by the time it hit the charts on November 7, Dorsey's premier attraction, Frank Sinatra, had been gone from the band's ranks almost two months. Before the split, Sinatra's contributions to the Dorsey discography, between mid-1941 and up to and including his final sessions in June and July the following year, offered proof-positive of his continuing improvement.

By 1942, Sinatra's singing had become poised, assured and appealing; with specific items, such as "There Are Such Things", "In The Blue Of Evening" and "It's Always You", you could detect a strong individual quality emerging. In terms of control, diction and phrasing, considerable progress was clearly evident. As close inspection of the contents of *Tommy Dorsey-Frank Sinatra: The Song Is You* confirms, Sinatra's talent had moved forward in a fascinating way.

MOVIES

Frank Sinatra's debut in movies remains shrouded in mystery. *Major Bowes' Amateur Theatre Off The Air* was the collective title for a series of shorts which were made in 1935. A 20-year-old Frank Sinatra is reported to have taken part in two or three. According to daughter Nancy, he played a waiter in the first – without being required to sing a note! – and was part of a minstrel show performance in the second.

As a member of the Dorsey band, he sang a tender "I'll Never Smile Again" in *Las Vegas Nights* (1941), a 90-minute Paramount release starring Constance Moore and Bert Wheeler among others. That brief appearance didn't make too much impact. As George T. Simon noted, "[He] sings prettily in an unphotogenic manner".

Sinatra had a little more to do in *Ship Ahoy!* (1942), when he was still with Tommy Dorsey. He featured in two new numbers – "Poor You", written by E. Y. Harburg and Burton Lane, and "The Last Call For Love", by Harburg, Lane and Margery Cummings – then, briefly, on the standard "Moonlight Bay", assisted by the Pied Pipers.

Sinatra takes a rest while leader Tommy Dorsey serenades Virginia O'Brien in *Ship Ahoy!*.

RADIO

From the early Forties onwards, Frank Sinatra's voice was introduced to millions of American radio listeners, who regularly checked in to broadcasts of the many big bands of the day.

With Harry James, there was limited scope for establishing a real reputation. The comparatively few broadcasts Sinatra did make with the James band during his six-month stay nevertheless provided an opportunity for a name check nationwide and for his voice to be introduced briefly to a large audience [*Harry James & His Orchestra: Bandstand Memories 1938 To 1948/ Harry James & His Orchestra Featuring Frank Sinatra: The Complete Recordings 1939*].

The gradual improvement in the emerging Sinatra vocal style continued throughout the Dorsey years. The best way of charting that progress is perhaps through the various airchecks which were broadcast over the years. For example, you can find some of these on the Tommy Dorsey-Frank Sinatra *The Song Is You* collection. They reveal a much more relaxed vocalist than the one heard on the Victor or Bluebird recordings – particularly those made during Sinatra's first year as a full-time pro.

Certainly, the radio versions of titles such as "Who?", "Once In A While", "How Am I To Know?" and "Yearning" – none of which were recorded commercially at the time – give some kind of indication of just how well, even in 1940, Sinatra must have come across in live performance. So, too, does Frank's version of the classic Jack Leonard feature, "Marie".

Even when the material featured as part of Dorsey's *Amateur Song Writing Program* was below par, there was no fall-off in the quality of Sinatra's singing. The same is true for albums compiled from radio collections such as *Tommy Dorsey And His Orchestra: Live At The Meadowbrook, February 11, 1941/August 18, 1942*.

GIGS

From the first tentative steps with Harry James to the final band-singing days with Tommy Dorsey, Sinatra made great strides as a live performer. There was a curiously detached quality to much of Sinatra's work with James. A most important ingredient in his singing – the feel, the projection of emotion – was hardly evident in the first commercial recordings, and there wasn't much improvement with those live performances, comprising radio remotes, that have now surfaced in album form.

The outstanding live item from the James years to emerge thus far is "All Or Nothing At All" from the 1939 World Fair. Like the commercial recording of the song made the previous month in August, this was the performance above all others that gave an indication of Sinatra's potential as a vocalist with real qualities of warmth and basic communication.

An impish looking Sinatra poses with fellow Dorsey band members at the Roseland Ballroom, 1939.

Like the forgettable "Vol Vistu Gaily Star" from the same broadcast, "All Or Nothing At All" first appeared as part of *One Night Stand With Harry James, Volume II*. More recently, there has been greater access to the Sinatra-James era with the appearance of *Harry James And His Orchestra: Bandstand Memories 1938 To 1948*. On this, you can hear the charm of the aspiring vocalist during a series of performances at the Roseland Ballroom. There are hints of better things to come from the vocals which grace such songs as "Star Dust", "My Love For You" and "This Is No Dream".

Sinatra's period with Dorsey is covered by a number of recordings now available. The Tommy Dorsey-Frank Sinatra album *The Song Is You* offers a comprehensive retrospective of those years: it ranges from the introspective vocalizing on "Who?", "I Hear A Rhapsody", "Once In A While", or the touching "I'll Never Smile Again", all from the singer's first year with Dorsey, to the more assured, convincing versions of "In The Blue Of Evening", "Just As Though You Were Here" and "The Song Is You", one of Sinatra's farewell offerings, all from 1942.

There are further examples of early Dorsey-Sinatra offerings on *Sinatra: The Radio Years 1939-55*, which contains such wistfully interpreted items as "I've Got My Eyes On You", "Polka Dots And Moonbeams", "Shadows On The Sand" and "That's How It Goes".

But Sinatra the Great Lyric Interpreter wasn't yet in full flower. That would happen when he became a fully-fledged solo artist …

Solo Sinatra

When Frank Sinatra quit the Tommy Dorsey band in Indianapolis, on September 10, 1942, his timing, it seemed, was just about right. By then, he'd served an eminently worthwhile apprentice-ship as vocalist with both the Harry James and Dorsey bands. Constant touring and playing had moulded Sinatra into a reliable performer, and he was just beginning to fulfil the great promise he had shown at the beginning of his career.

Dick Haymes – a marvellous balladeer and another big threat to Crosby.

During the four dues-paying years between 1939 and 1942, Sinatra's learning curve had been impressive and it was set to continue on an upward spiral. Year by year, he had grown in confidence – especially during the latter half of the Dorsey period. Improvement was most noticeable in the way Sinatra could project a wide variety of songs with unflappable ease – by 1942, the way he put his material across was truly convincing.

Sinatra had yet to become the legendary lyric interpreter of later years, but there was no doubting the care he took to make even the least eloquent lyrics sound as if they contained a ring of truth. In terms of technique, control and sensitivity, Sinatra's overall method of delivery was, by 1942, beginning to impress even the Doubting Thomases among the critics, who had hitherto remained unmoved: their reviews tended to concentrate on the uninhibited reactions of adoring young female fans, who clustered round the stand during a typical Sinatra feature with Dorsey.

Sinatra – *the* classic MGM mug shot that said it all . . .

Leaving Dorsey when he did was a shrewd move for another important reason – it kept Sinatra ahead of the pack. For weeks, he'd known through the big band grapevine that rival singers Dick Haymes, his successor with both Harry James and Tommy Dorsey, Perry Como (Ted Weems), as well as Jimmy Dorsey's long-serving vocalist, Bob Eberly, were also planning to go solo. And, probably unbeknownst to the other four, Earl Hines' tall-and-handsome vocalist, Billy Eckstine, wanted to follow suit.

In fact, when granted his release from Tommy Dorsey, it was Dick Haymes who proved to be the principal threat to Sinatra's ascendancy; first, in the record charts, then as a highly-personable movie personality. Perry Como would take just a little longer to establish himself with record buyers of the early-Forties – but not that long.

Bob Eberly, alas, would never make the big time … even though he'd built a considerable following with the Jimmy Dorsey Orchestra, from 1936 to 1943, and had been featured on no fewer than nine chart-topping hits, two sharing credits with Helen

O'Connell. Eberly's early popularity had brought him third place among the top pop vocalists in the annual *Billboard* college polls, between 1940 and 1943, but his career proper was interrupted by military service. Even though he wangled himself a posting to Chicago, where he worked with an orchestra fronted by (Captain) Wayne King, following discharge, he never fully established himself as a big name solo performer. Eberly's post-war career ran to a trio of minor hit recordings, leadership for a while of his own big bands and appearances (sometimes reunited with O'Connell) at nostalgia-based concerts.

Career-wise, Billy Eckstine's development took much longer than the others, due to his whole-hearted commitment to fronting a legendary jazz orchestra. This has since been recognized as one of the most exciting outfits in the whole of big band jazz history: the band was the crucible for a whole, new and revolutionary kind of jazz called either bebop or rebop; ultimately, simply bop.

Band membership comprised many future giants of the genre, including, at various times, such luminaries as Charlie Parker, Dizzy Gillespie, Fats Navarro, Dexter Gordon, Sonny Stitt, Gene Ammons and the ever-present Art Blakey. Sarah Vaughan shared vocals with leader Eckstine – but it was his more-or-less straight ballad singing which achieved any kind of commercial viability for this remarkable unit. These musicians were light years ahead of their time and just what the ballroom types, who normally followed Glenn Miller and the Dorseys, – let alone fans of the Mickey Mouse bands like King, Sammy Kaye and Kyser! – made of them is almost beyond comprehension. That the band lasted for as long as it did (1944–47) was due entirely to Eckstine's dedication; even before the inevitable

The doubly talented Billy Eckstine, band leader-cum-balladeer.

One black vocalist was receiving ever-increasing acceptance at this time – namely, Nat King Cole. Singing was just one of his talents: to the jazz-minded, he was one of the music's most gifted and influential keyboard players; for others, his personal appeal lay within the context of the King Cole Trio, whose repertoire – an important aspect of the combo's growing popularity – included a crowd-pleasing mix of standards and current ballads, jump tunes, R&B originals, novelties … and an acceptable form of basic jazz that was scarcely likely to offend the non-jazzers. But Nat King Cole's reputation as a major solo singer was not to be consolidated until the end of the Forties. That was when he disbanded the Trio in exchange for a less jazz-based band, designed to give his recordings a bigger sound …

The Nat King Cole Trio.

crunch came, he was up to his neck in personal debt.

Even without the numerous near disasters that dogged his bandleading career, it is impossible to say whether Eckstine on his own could have competed with the likes of Sinatra and Dick Haymes. The truth is that Eckstine would have been one of precious few black solo vocalists to venture into what was then a white-oriented world of popular entertainment. And, with the exception of a small handful of performers (e.g. Duke Ellington, Louis Armstrong, Ethel Waters and Cab Calloway), the prospects for black superstardom during this period were distinctly unpromising.

For Frank Sinatra, though, the future looked full of promise. For one thing, he had eyes for Hollywood and wanted to conquer the silver screen. He had also become **Frank had eyes for** increasingly aware of the importance of **Hollywood – aware of** radio, and his ambitions were no longer **radio's importance –** limited to guest-spot appearances on **but a major problem** other people's programmes – he **arose with record** wanted a regular show of his own. **plans.**

Supreme confidence in his own ability – a confidence bordering on outright arrogance – gave him every reason to believe that, sooner rather than later, he would be accorded his own sponsored radio series: one that would rival Bing Crosby's widely popular *Kraft Music Hall* series, which had been continually on the air since 1935. Thanks to the brash and cocky mentality that had helped him survive two and a half years of non-stop singing with the Tommy Dorsey Band, there was little or no doubt in Sinatra's mind that he would soon be recognized as the world's leading vocal performer, both in concert and on the nightclub scene.

However, a major problem arose in a crucial area which held up Sinatra and his rivals for a long time. On August 1, 1942, following a dispute over musicians' royalty payments and through the unstinting efforts of its ruthless, much-feared president, James Petrillo, the powerful American Federation of Musicians instituted a blanket ban on recording activities by musicians. Singers, however, were allowed to record – even though they could only perform in a strictly solo capacity or, alternatively, utilize the services of an established vocal group or specially assembled chorus. For Sinatra, Columbia chose the latter.

A strike ensued and remained solid, with neither side willing to make concessions. The dispute finished, to all intents and purposes, some thirteen months later when the union came to an agreement through Petrillo and his officers that satisfied all the record companies, except the two largest: Victor and Columbia. They held out for a further 14 months before they too agreed terms and contracts were signed on November 11, 1944.

Sinatra must have been particularly upset because, thanks to the personal intercession of the company's chief A&R man Manie Sachs, he had chosen to sign with Columbia after leaving Dorsey: Sachs had continued to be impressed with Sinatra's progress, since first hearing him on-stage over a year before the split. He and Sinatra were to become good friends and, under Sachs' wise guidance, the Columbia association started well – despite the fact that Frank Sinatra was not allowed to employ the services of the man who was to be his closest and most important musical associate for the next ten years. At least, though, Axel Stordahl's brilliant conducting and arranging skills could still enhance Sinatra's singing on radio and in Hollywood movies during the period of the AFM ban. Sachs' influence and judgement would continue until 1950,

All-star radio: Django Reinhardt, Claudette Colbert, Frank, Bing, at the Hollywood Canteen, 1945.

when he left to join Victor. But the personal friendship lasted until the A&R man's death in 1959 at the age of just 53.

After Frank Sinatra split from the Dorsey band in 1942, he went to the West Coast to check out Hollywood and his prospects in motion pictures. As pianist-arranger-bandleader Skitch Henderson told journalist George T. Simon, Sinatra had visions of landing a staff singing post at NBC in the movie capital.

There was, however, to be no NBC post. Instead, Sinatra was drafted into the cast of the movie, *Reveille With Beverly*, a run-of-the-mill production from Columbia Pictures. The movie was little more than an excuse to parade the musical talents of top bands (Duke Ellington, Count Basie, Bob Crosby and Freddie Slack), vocalists (apart from Sinatra, Ella Mae Morse and the Mills Brothers) and the impressive terpsichorean skills of dancer Ann

Miller. Surrounded by a bevy of Hollywood lovelies, Sinatra sang a poised, sincerely felt "Night And Day". Being the briefest of movie debuts, though, his was scarcely a riveting performance.

Sinatra soon returned to New York, where, thanks to Manie Sachs, he joined the list of clients at the powerful GAC agency. To pay the bills, he did a CBS radio show for five months, starting in October. This, in turn, led to involvement with the Lucky Strike-sponsored *Your Hit Parade*, which began in February 1943.

But it was a remarkable series of gigs which brought Sinatra's biggest breakthrough: remarkable as much for the way the audience went wild as for any brilliance on the part of the singer. Again, it was Manie Sachs who engineered things. He obtained a booking for Frank at the Mosque Theater, a large hall of entertainment in Newark, New Jersey. Then, Sachs invited along Bob Weitman, the managing director of the prestigious Paramount Theater. Impressed as he was by Sinatra's singing, Weitman was astounded by the near-hysterical reaction of the predominantly youthful audience.

The very next day, Weitman called Benny Goodman, who was the headline act at the Paramount, and told him that he was attaching Frank Sinatra as an "extra added attraction" to the bill. Goodman's only comment was: "Who's he?" The King of Swing was soon to find out. But, for the opening show on December 30, 1942, Goodman confined himself to introducing the newcomer in a way that was brief and to the point,

"And now, Frank Sinatra ..."

Even before the young singer stepped on-stage, the roar of anticipation from the teenage audience was deafening. Both Sinatra and Goodman stood rooted to the spot as if paralyzed. First to recover, the bandleader turned around, faced the perpetrators of the noise and inquired of no one in particular, "What the fuck is that?" Sinatra laughed, relaxed and ambled his way out to centre-stage. Following this, he gave what George T. Simon later described as a "tremendously effective show".

Benny sings Sinatra, Frank plays Goodman – the two giants have fun on Sinatra's radio show.

The "that" to which Goodman referred with such genuine incredulity was, of course, the "official" opening of the Bobbysox Era. It was also the beginning of an amazing period in Sinatra's eventful show business career, when mass adulation – particularly from young women but by no means restricted to one gender – reached its first peak.

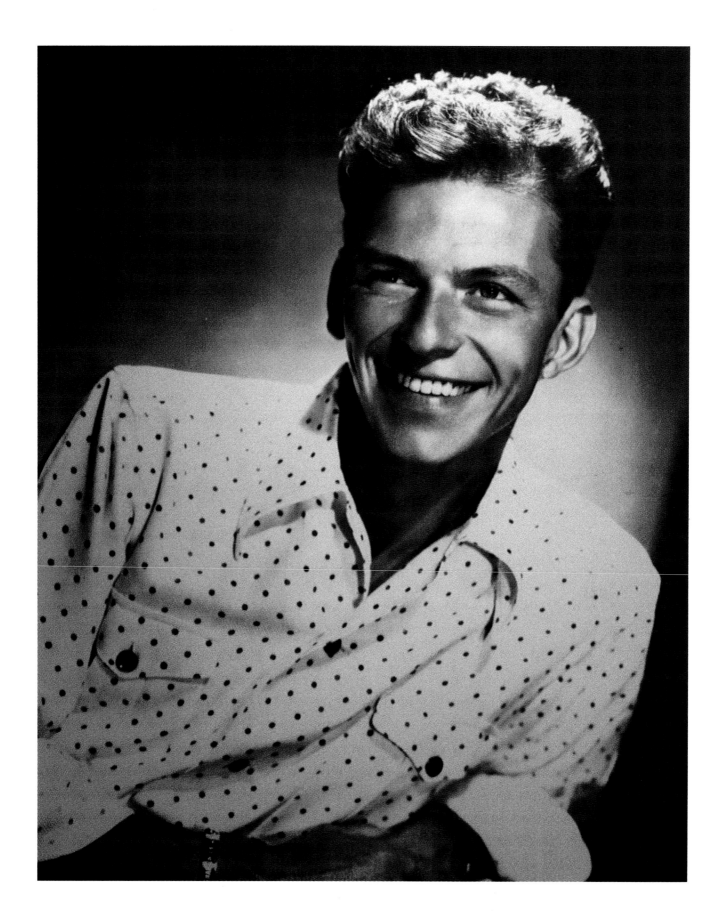

Measured against previous outbreaks of mass hero-worship in the US, this kind of uninhibited fan frenzy far outstripped anything previously accorded to matinee idols Rudolph Valentino and Rudy Vallee (even allowing for the fact that, generally speaking, the age group of those idolaters made them rather more grown-up). This kind of adulation – the tears, the fainting, the screams – was not to be seen again until the arrival on the pop scene at the beginning of the Fifties of the Nabob of Sob, Johnny Ray.

Later, pop idols such as Elvis Presley, the Beatles, the Rolling Stones, and teenyboppers such as David Cassidy, the Osmonds (individually and collectively) and the Jackson Five, exerted the same near-hypnotic effect on predominantly teenage admirers. In more recent times, Michael Jackson, Prince and Madonna have elicited the same kind of reaction from literally millions of their faithful flock, worldwide.

After this sensational opening, Sinatra and Goodman continued in tandem for the rest of the one-month booking. Weitman was so utterly delighted with Sinatra's Paramount debut that he offered the new Number One vocal heart-throb a further month's appearances immediately after the first batch was completed. It took the eager Sinatra seconds to say "Yes". During the second month, accompaniment was provided by the orchestras of Sonny Dunham and Johnny Long. Meanwhile, Goodman, complete with Orchestra and Sextet, plus young blonde vocalist Peggy Lee, had departed to fulfil previous engagements.

Critic George T. Simon had followed Sinatra's progress throughout the band-singing period, and so it came as no surprise when he put in an appearance at the Sinatra-Goodman season. His review was enthusiastic. "He could have stayed on indefinitely, but he didn't …" And, continued Simon, the most memorable individual performance of the evening was his tender version of "She's Funny That Way", the Richard Whiting-Neil Moret classic published in 1928, which Sinatra had probably heard sung by Billie Holiday on 52nd Street. For the Paramount performance of this number Frank was supported only by

Goodman's pianist, Jess Stacy, a particularly effective way of presenting a ballad that was to become a Sinatra specialty in concert for the rest of his career.

As Sinatra's extended season at the Paramount continued and the crowds grew larger, the adolescent screams and shrieks grew louder and more insistent. Weitman engaged extra guards to maintain order. Even then, some girls refused to leave their seats after the show, insisting on remaining where they were until the following morning. Some fainted – either from the excitement of seeing their hero on stage, or from hunger because they hadn't been able to eat.

Many people remained unmoved by the furore surrounding Sinatra. They found it difficult to understand what such a large percentage of teenage America saw in the thin, gangling Frank Sinatra of the bobbysox days; even today, there are those who still cannot relate to any of the explanations given. The way they saw it, Sinatra was hardly in the same league as movie heart-throbs of the early Forties – Gable, Taylor, Power, et al. In their eyes, he seriously lacked machismo. And the sometimes limp-fitting suits he wore, the floppy bow-ties and the tousled hair that occasionally fell over his forehead, together hardly seemed to add up to Sinatra the Sex Symbol.

But sex symbol Sinatra was, without a doubt. On stage, he possessed an indefinable kind of magnetism that was apparent even to certain grown-ups, who, out of perverse curiosity, turned up at his concerts. Cool, confident Sinatra certainly knew how to play up his sexual side in the way he moved, and how to seduce the audience with a sudden intake of breath, or a smile, or by a deliberate gesture with a free hand. His voice was sexy, too. Time and again, he would bring increased screams and shouts from his audiences by deliberately extending a single word, or stressing a certain phrase: "I'm not much to look at, nothin' to see …", from "She's Funny That Way", inevitably brought forth a torrent of protests, in the vein of:

"No-o-o, Frankie-ee! You're gorgeous … You're super …"

Reviewers, who deigned to attend a Sinatra performance, tended not to agree that Frankie was gorgeous. Invariably, few words were wasted on Sinatra's actual singing; instead, reviews concentrated on deprecating the star's negative influence on youngsters, as well as deploring the manner in which he could manipulate their emotions. Needless to say, there were few kind words for his mode of dress either. But one publication at least conceded that, in the flesh, Sinatra possessed charisma. A reviewer for *Time* magazine declared,

"Not since Rudolph Valentino has American womanhood made such unabashed public love to an entertainer."

After the successful launch of his Lucky Strike-sponsored radio show in February 1943, came Sinatra's first involvement with the night-club circuit, an area where he would find few, if any, rivals in succeeding years ... let alone anyone to surpass him.

On March 17, Sinatra began a season at the Riobamba Club, located on West 57th Street, Manhattan. Originally pencilled in as second string to veteran comedian Walter O'Keefe, Frank Sinatra was an instant smash hit. Not only did he produce top-quality singing, but he also continued to pack in customers during a four-week engagement. Night after night, the reaction of the Riobamba audiences was genuinely enthusiastic. So pleased was the club's manager that the original weekly fee of $750 was hiked to $1,000, well before the month had been completed. By the time the season had been extended – and then re-extended – that weekly figure had risen by another $500.

After the Riobamba triumph, Sinatra was booked into Frank Dailey's Meadowbrook nightspot. Once again, he scored with SRO (Sold Right Out) audiences, some of whom had come along specifically to mock this skinny young man – who looked much younger than his 28 years – and put him in his place. Then, in May, came a return to the Paramount. And now his weekly salary had risen from $2,100 to a princely $3,100 ...

The new king of the nightclub singers. Sinatra won over even the hardest-to-please audience, and silenced the noisiest drunk.

By the fall, Frank Sinatra was appearing in the plush Wedgwood Room at the distinctly upmarket Waldorf-Astoria, New York. Now, there could be no doubt whatsoever that he had truly hit the big time. The only negative moment of the Waldorf-Astoria season came one evening, when an obviously drunk customer lurched to his feet and bawled out loudly, "You stink!" Stopping in mid-song, Frank strode purposefully from the stage and invited the drunk outside. The offer was refused, without a word being offered in reply.

Returning to the stage, Sinatra addressed the audience. "Ladies and gentlemen, I like to sing. I'm paid to sing. Those who don't like my voice are not compelled to come and surely are under no obligation to stay." There was spontaneous applause.

That Sinatra could perform just as impressively outdoors had been confirmed almost two months before the Wedgwood Room gig.

On August 14, 1943, he succeeded in packing the Hollywood Bowl on his first appearance there. Morris Stoloff, the film

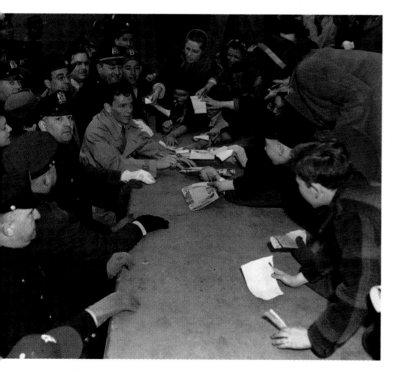

Frank signs for the fans at a Red Cross fundraising event at Ebbetsfield in 1944.

composer-arranger, conducted for him. And Sinatra was astonished by the volume, as well as the genuine warmth, of applause he received from a capacity audience of West Coast fans.

To all but those without ears to hear, there was no doubt that Sinatra was now a superb singer.

But even more extraordinary fan-reaction was to follow in October 1944, after the announcement of a further Paramount booking: this time, the tumultuous reception was not confined within any one venue. It all started when Sinatra arrived for a 6 am rehearsal on the first day of the engagement and was startled to observe almost a thousand bobbysox girls waiting outside the theatre. Despite a 9 pm curfew for juveniles – imposed by Mayor LaGuardia – police maintained that queues had begun to form at three in the morning. By seven, the main queue stretched down to Eighth Avenue. When the theatre opened at 8.30 am, all 3,600 seats were filled.

A new movie – *Our Hearts Were Young And Gay*, starring Gail Russell, Diana Lynn, Charles Ruggles and Dorothy Gish – which preceded the Sinatra appearance, backed by the Raymond Paige Orchestra, was completely ignored. The bobbysoxers chatted and chanted their hero's name throughout its duration. When, finally, he appeared, all hell was let loose.

The next day – Columbus Day and a school holiday to boot – saw even more amazing scenes. Approximately 10,000 youngsters queued six-abreast outside the auditorium, with another huge crowd, estimated at 20,000, jamming Times Square. There were numerous fainting incidents, some injuries, minor vandalism – and several arrests. Vast numbers of police reinforcements were called in to control these remarkable scenes. Even so, they were easily outnumbered and absolutely powerless to do anything about dispersing the crowd.

Inside the Paramount, hundreds of young girls refused to leave their seats after the first show – some managed to stay for two, or even three, performances. And such was the ferocity of their adulation that, on the third day, an 18-year-old boy was almost lynched by a gang of incensed females, after he'd thrown an egg with admirable accuracy at Sinatra during his rendition of "I Don't Know Why". On stage, Sinatra himself had to be protected from the attentions of his rabid fans. Their single-minded attempts to claw at his hair, clothes or bow-ties required

the combined energy of the law and his own personal bodyguards to prevent physical damage.

The bobbysox phenomenon lasted for several years. During that time, it succeeded in dividing the young from the old. Many thousands of words were written by journalists, music critics, the clergy and even leading psychoanalysts in all manner of publications to explain the "problem". The explanations given were numerous and wildly differing, sometimes bizarre. For some medical pundits, it was due to "war-time degeneracy", to others it was all "a product of the maternal urge to feed the hungry".

There was also much media speculation about the causes of such extraordinary events as "The Columbus Day Riot", as the incident henceforth became known, and how much it was down to the natural (or even unnatural) instincts of pubescence. But here most commentators were overlooking the exceptional PR skills of one George B. Evans …

George B. Evans became Frank Sinatra's press agent in 1942. During the next six years, he made himself absolutely indispensable to the singer in keeping the name "Sinatra" on every front page – and, just as importantly, defending the star against numerous press attacks on his character.

Many of these accusations appear to have been well-founded. It was Evans, for instance, who worked wonders in muting the possibility of the worst kind of personal publicity. This followed a succession of extra-marital affairs that threatened to blow apart Sinatra's cleancut-family-man image, which the PR man constantly stressed in his hand-outs and personal conversations with newspaper journalists. It was Evans' skill, too, that helped reduce the publicity which automatically surrounded Sinatra's outbursts in public – often violent outbursts – which were invariably aimed at reporters and photographers. And, of course, in the first place, it had been Evans, whose untiring efforts helped ignite the bobbysox phenomenon, then continued to fan the flames of publicity, which inevitably led to the Columbus Day episode.

Despite continued scepticism in some quarters of the critical fraternity, Sinatra's vocal talent endured.

In a strictly PR context, Evans' greatest achievements surrounded events at the Paramount Theater. No doubt of that. His highly imaginative scams involved not only whipping up frenzy among scores of teenage girls, but manipulation of Sinatra himself. For example, Evans suggested to Sinatra that caressing the microphone (the stand-up variety) would elicit an excited response from young women in the audience. So, too, would the occasional swaying of the slim frame, with or without mike.

If Sinatra held his arms wide open, when he sang the phrase

"Come to Papa, come to Papa, do …"

from the Gershwin standard, "Embraceable You", it would bring front-row teenyboppers to yell, "Oh, Daddy!", the reply which Evans had planted earlier. A little further coaching from Evans induced some girls to faint, and others to moan loudly.

Frank Sinatra with Ava Gardner, an affair that went the whole distance – into marriage.

On Columbus Day, a school holiday, Evans gave away hundreds of free tickets for the Paramount shows. Nevertheless, later, he always fiercely denied stage-managing subsequent events in the street outside the Paramount Theater. However, he never denied sweet-talking the leading booking agency for the nation's symphony orchestras into allowing his client to play a series of concerts – at Lewisohn Stadium, New York, the Hollywood Bowl and at Washington, DC, utilizing four leading classical ensembles – so that those venues' poor box-office receipts would be given a much-needed financial boost.

Although heavy press criticism of events surrounding Sinatra's personal performances tended to overshadow other professional commitments, Frank Sinatra was still making his name as a recording artist. Despite the absence of arranger Axel Stordahl, the first five *a cappella* studio sessions – held in New York, between June and November 1943 – demonstrated yet again that the decision to go it alone was the right one.

With Alec Wilder providing high-quality choral arrangements – and no doubt adding words of wisdom to an anxious Sinatra – and the backgrounds handled with predictable expertise by a selection of top session vocalists, led by Bobby Tucker, the results, from Sinatra's standpoint, were promising.

Even though there were moments when his singing tended to lack total conviction, there was no doubt that Sinatra was hitting the spot in terms of sincerity, sensitivity and musicality. His approach to lyrics showed an attention to detail that would become part-and-parcel of his future recording work. The diction was faultless. The phrasing was elegant. The control very good. And there was no lacking in feel – even though the depth of expression had yet to reach the level of his Columbia recordings from 1944 and thereafter ... and, of course, which Sinatra raised to optimum level in his post-Columbia years.

In terms of artistic development, Sinatra's work as a recording artist stayed well ahead of his career in films. The same can be said of his rapid growth as a live performer.

As far as Hollywood was concerned, the studios didn't care about the quality of characters Sinatra had to play on screen during his first five years – inevitably, they would be the warm, smiling, likeable type. Naturally, in the film companies' eyes, Sinatra was first and foremost a singer. However, no matter what kind of nonsensical story or setting was involved, there was thankfully scope for The Voice to deliver the goods. And, usually, Sinatra was well-served by the material written for his movies, which he made initially for RKO, then MGM, after signing a highly lucrative contract with the latter.

Frank's radio series presented talents like the delicious young Jane Powell.

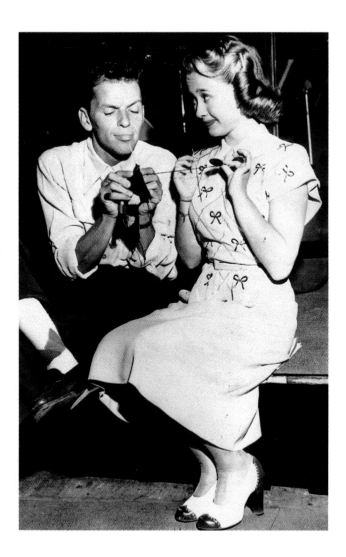

Harold Adamson and Jimmy McHugh were the songwriters for *Higher And Higher*, Sinatra's first full-length motion picture. For *Step Lively*, the team of Sammy Cahn and Jule Styne was brought in to produce new material. Between 1943 and 1951, the same combination of talents was involved in *Anchors Aweigh!*, *It Happened In Brooklyn* and *Double Dynamite*. Film critics gave a collective thumbs-up to the on-screen vocals – albeit, in some cases, grudgingly – but few were over-impressed by Sinatra's potential in the acting stakes.

Sinatra's progress in conquering the US airwaves ran parallel with his successes on record. The most important early developments in these vital areas related to his obtaining top billing on the prestigious *Your Hit Parade* radio series, which he contributed to for two separate runs, and, finally his very own series, *Songs By Sinatra*.

Both on radio and on record, his work was of consistent high quality. And there were few, if any, complaints about his concert or club appearances. Whether performing at the Hollywood Bowl or at the Waldorf-Astoria, Sinatra's stature as an artist kept growing throughout the Forties and, well before the decade was out, he was acknowledged as king of the live performers.

Towards the end of the Forties, though, a noticeable decline set in. His often tempestuous personal private life didn't help. Still less did his torrid romance with Ava Gardner, known to magazine readers as the Most Beautiful Woman In The World. While this affair was going on, the gradual disintegration of his marriage with Nancy gave the press ample opportunity to put Sinatra's life under the microscope.

Perhaps foolishly, Sinatra gave them plenty of ammunition with which to bombard his personal reputation. The attacks and counter-attacks continued to accelerate alarmingly as members of the press from all over the world pursued Sinatra and Gardner relentlessly, wherever they went.

Sinatra's popularity slumped disastrously and this was reflected by a marked decrease in sales of his records. Reviews, too, were often less kind than hitherto. Ratings for the *Light Up Time* radio series began to worry its sponsors. By the beginning of 1952, there were rumours that the days of *The Frank Sinatra Show*, on television, were numbered. And the movies weren't pulling in the punters as before …

Every picture tells a story ... A dejected Frank Sinatra stares into space.

Already, some critics were sharpening their knives. The obituaries were being prepared.

1943-1952

RECORDS

FROM HIS VERY FIRST solo Columbia recordings, it was obvious that Sinatra was ready to launch himself as a vocalist in his own right.

True, there was an occasional hesitancy in those first *a cappella* sessions, but this could no doubt be put down to the absence of Axel Stordahl's arranging skills – the American Federation of Musicians had banned musicians from taking part in recording until a new agreement over royalties was reached. Even so, composer and arranger Alec Wilder had rehearsed the mixed chorus into performing excellently as a kind of surrogate background in place of the band.

Even at this early stage in his career, Sinatra was something of a perfectionist inside a recording studio. This is perhaps best illustrated by the fact that he cut three separate versions of "People Will Say We're In Love" before, finally, he was satisfied. Two versions were also made of "The Music Stopped". In this case, **Rehearsals don't** however, both takes were to remain on **always have to be** the shelf until the Sixties, before they **a drag.** received a first-time release. Whatever

misgivings there may have been about accompaniments, Sinatra's new recordings sold in large numbers. Even though Dick Haymes copped top spot on the Hit Parade with "You'll Never Know", Sinatra took the same song to Number 2; "People Will Say We're In Love" peaked at 3; "Couldn't Sleep A Wink Last Night" at 4; "Sunday, Monday, Or Always" at 9; and "Lovely Way To Spend An Evening" failed by just one place to make the Top 10.

At all five of the all-ballad *a cappella* sessions, there was a high level of artistic consistency in Sinatra's vocals, which augured well for recordings once the union ban was over. With Stordahl finally in harness, further improvement seemed guaranteed. And that's how it went at the very next Columbia session, almost exactly one year after the final date with Wilder and the Bobby Tucker Singers.

Backed by a 35-piece orchestra including nineteen strings (and featuring a harp), there was a real authority to Sinatra's singing. Stordahl's writing was exquisite – as it remained throughout the Columbia years. A beautifully felt version of "White Christmas" made it to the Top 10. Today, more than fifty years later, "Saturday Night (Is The Loneliest Night of the Week)", his first real rhythmic excursion on record, still sounds pretty good. It proved irresistible to his fans and, like "You'll Never Know", only missed out being Sinatra's first chart-topper by one place.

When you listen to the magnificent 1993-released 12-CD boxed set, *Frank Sinatra: The Complete Columbia Recordings, 1943–1952*, the level of vocal performance – thanks, of course, to the presence of Stordahl – is excellent proof not only of Sinatra's consistency, but also of the fact that he continued to set higher and higher standards for other singers to keep up with.

In the whole, wide field of popular music, Sinatra was the greatest vocal performer of his era – even allowing for the fact that Crosby never sounded better than during the Forties, or that Haymes, Como and Eckstine were likewise coming into their prime.

During this period, Sinatra recorded prolifically, yet, time and again, managed to turn out absolute gems. It would be tedious to mention them all, but the list of classics must include "Mam'selle" (the last of three Hit Parade Number 1 successes), "White Christmas", "Nancy", "Ol' Man River", "Embraceable You" (in many ways, the archetypal Frank Sinatra song of the Forties), "She's Funny That Way", "Where Or When", "The Things We Did Last Summer", a two-part "Soliloquy" from *Carousel* (his first solo 12-inch disc release), "Time After Time", "Always", "But Beautiful", "I've Got A Crush On You" (with sensitive trumpet obbligato/solo from Bobby Hackett) and "Why Was I Born?".

There were other outstanding delights around this time, including a one-off jazz date as a member of the 1946 Metronome All Stars, who included Coleman Hawkins, Johnny Hodges, Nat Cole and Buddy Rich, with Sinatra taking a chorus-and-half of "Sweet Lorraine" in appropriate loose-swinging fashion. Another one-off delight featured a duet with the legendary Pearl Bailey, "A Little Learnin' Is A Dangerous Thing". Sinatra handled his part – repartee and all – remarkably well in such formidable company.

In more conventional mode, Sinatra's finest individual moments came on July 30, 1945. Sinatra empathized brilliantly with his collaborator, Axel Stordahl, who had produced some of his most sensitive writing for a nine-piece chamber-style ensemble with just three strings. His phrasing and feel on "Someone To Watch Over

Me", "These Foolish Things" and "I Don't Know Why" are well-nigh flawless. Pride of place, however, goes to the definitive treatment of "You Go To My Head", which is as near to perfection, vocally and instrumentally, as you could ever get. In fact, the entire output from the three-chamber styled sessions – ten titles in all, issued as five separate discs – would be collated as Frank's first ever 78 rpm album. Futuristically, its overall concept and mood looked forward to the classsic Capitol long-playing set, *Close To You*.

The post-1947 Columbia work tends to show not only a slow decline in Sinatra's vocal powers, but also reflects the myriad of personal and professional problems – sometimes quite vividly. Most revealing is his first recording of "I'm A Fool To Want You", with Sinatra sharing lyric-writing credits with composers Jack

Radio giant CBS networked both *Your Hit Parade* and *Songs By Sinatra*.

Wolf and Joel Herron. George T. Simon has called it "the most moving side Sinatra has ever recorded". Even today it sounds like a genuine *cri de coeur* to Ava Gardner. In its own less gut-level way, his revival of the standard "Love Me", recorded at the same date, imparts an undeniable emotional depth: this time, though, delivered strictly and poignantly *sotto voce*.

These last two songs were made during the infamous Mitch Miller period (Miller had taken over from Manie Sachs as A&R man at Columbia). So, even if the gimmicks and totally inappropriate material of this time tend to be remembered most of all, Miller did at least supervise one session which produced worthwhile Sinatra material. Perhaps the worst example of "Mitch Millerism" was the excruciating "Mama Will Bark", with European cabaret artist Dagmar contributing nothing towards a disastrous concoction, even with studio man Donald Bain's canine noises in the background.

vocal contributions. No commercial recordings were made of "Come Out, Come Out, Wherever You Are", " As Long As There's Music" or "Some Other Time" (arguably, the best), or "Where Does Love Begin?", although V-Disc versions now exist in CD format of the first and third: *The V-Discs: The Columbia Years 1943–1952*.

Anchors Aweigh! (MGM, 1945) has even finer Sinatra vocals. It was his first high-profile movie – the first of three he would make with Gene Kelly and his first in sailor-boy suit, but the third with Stordahl's unmistakable vocal arrangements – and everyone came out of it well, including Sinatra. Vocally, he sounded more assured and convincing than ever. Cahn and Styne had come up with five more numbers, including a particularly appealing Sinatra–Gene Kelly duet ("I Begged Her"). Finest of the quintet, though, were a tender "The Charm Of You" and, in particular, a yearning rendition of "I Fall In Love Too Easily", with Sinatra seated in front of a grand piano on stage at an empty Hollywood Bowl.

The 10 minute-long *The House I Live In* (RKO, 1945) received a Special Award from the Academy of Motion Picture Arts And Sciences for its plea for racial tolerance, a message that Sinatra delivered with sincerity and no Hollywood-type falsehood. Musically, he handled "If You Are But A Dream" and the heavily patriotic "The House I Live In" with a similar lack of melodrama. The critics were impressed. If only they'd closed their eyes, they might have appreciated just how impressive a job Sinatra made of "Ol' Man River" – used as the climax of *Till The Clouds Roll By* (1946), MGM's star-studded Jerome Kern biopic. Unfortunately, the image of Frank Sinatra, clad all in white, perched atop a white dais and surrounded by an all-white orchestra and chorus, stands forever as Hollywood at its bad-taste worst.

It Happened In Brooklyn (MGM, 1946) found Sinatra switching from navy-blue to khaki to play a GI returning home from war. His acting at last gave hints of a promising, if underdeveloped, talent – helped unquestionably by the presence of Jimmy Durante alongside him. But the singing still took centre stage.

Higher and Higher: Frank – nice, friendly young man, exuding appealing boy-next-door charm.

A duet between Sinatra and Durante, "The Song's Gotta Come From The Heart", remains a delightful excursion into vaudeville. It was just one of five new Cahn–Styne creations, which included Sinatra on his own sounding wistful on

"It's The Same Old Dream", happy-go-lucky on "I Believe" and especially persuasive with "Time After Time". Less important are a tentative stab at Mozart, "La Ci Darem La Mano" – a typical "touch of class", Hollywood-style – and Sinatra's version of the traditional "Black Eyes", sung in his own special brand of Russian.

A few more song writing contributions from Cahn and Styne might have made *The Miracle Of The Bells* (RKO, 1948) a tad more bearable. This strictly non-musical

Sinatra impressed the critics as well as his fans with *The House I Live In*.

non-event had Sinatra donning clerical garb as a Roman Catholic priest with but one song to perform. It was another imported number, "Ever Homeward" – anglicized by Cahn, polished by Styne – sung in both its original Polish and English. But as for acting, there was nothing to write home about …

Sinatra's only role of note came in the film that book-ended the decade: *Meet Danny Wilson* (Universal International, 1951). Even so, the movie was primarily a musical with Sinatra more or less playing himself. The plot was traditional: a singer, who is trying to make it, is befriended then stitched up by a racketeer night-club owner. There were more songs than Sinatra had sung in any previous movie, all but one standards. These included "She's Funny That Way", "How Deep Is The Ocean?", "That

Old Black Magic" and "I've Got A Crush On You" … and they betrayed little trace of any decline in Sinatra's vocal powers.

In between *Miracle Of The Bells* and *Meet Danny Wilson* was sandwiched a diverse selection of average-to-good, poor and downright terrible films. Most definitely in the latter category was the excruciating *The Kissing Bandit* (MGM, 1948), about which nothing further need be said.

Take Me Out To The Ball Game (MGM, 1949) was a reunion with Gene Kelly and concerned a couple of vaudevillians, who also excel at baseball. Although directed by the legendary Busby Berkeley, it failed to take off. All but two numbers have Sinatra sharing vocals with Kelly and co-stars Betty Garrett, Jules Munshin and Esther Williams. Sung alone, "She's The Right Girl for Me" is pure Sinatra. Regrettably, "Boys And Girls Like You And Me" was left on the cutting room floor. For years, copies of the soundtrack version of this number have circulated among collectors. However, the laser disc version of *That's Entertainment* includes the missing sequence – which was apparently found only in 1993 – in all its glory …

Double Dynamite (RKO, 1951) is a touch better than *The Kissing Bandit,* but that isn't saying a lot. Even the usually enlivening presence of Groucho Marx can scarcely inject life

On The Town – classic Hollywood, classic Sinatra and Kelly.

into this Irving Cummings-directed flop. Messrs Cahn and Styne produced two of their least effective numbers, which Sinatra performed efficiently, in duet with Marx on "It's Only Money" and with Jane Russell on "Kisses And Tears". Sinatra actually recorded this last song twice – first as a solo performance (1949), then with Russell and the Modernaires (1950).

Take Me Out To The Ball Game – Sinatra, Gene Kelly, Esther Williams and Betty Garrett.

Of all the Sinatra musicals of the Forties the one that will be remembered most fondly is MGM's classic *On The Town* (1949). It was to be Sinatra's last collaboration with Gene Kelly (who co-directed with Stanley Donen) and it also reunited him with Garrett and Munshin from *Take Me Out To The Ball Game.* Sinatra's overall performance matched the rest of the cast in terms of exuberance and sheer *joie de vivre.* Once again, he was cast as the hapless if likeable sailor who nevertheless finds romance with the vivacious Garrett, cast this time as a wisecracking New York taxi-driver. Sinatra shared the song allocation with the other leading characters in various permutations, including the spirited opening "New York, New York", "Count On Me" and the title tune. Best of all, though, is "You're Awful", a charming duet with Garrett.

RADIO

SINATRA'S GROWING STATURE in the field of radio matched his success in live performance and the encouraging sales of his first solo recordings. Of course, radio could never hope to equal the glamour of the silver screen, or be as accessible as the gramophone record in the purchaser's home and heart. Nevertheless, radio was a powerful medium for any performer and Sinatra was fortunate to be given many opportunities to parade his talent on the airwaves throughout the next five years and beyond.

There were many guest appearances on shows which catered for huge audiences, such as *Here's To The Veterans, Personal Album, Mail Call* and *Something For The Girls* – many of these were transcribed and re-broadcast by the Armed Forces Radio Service. The AFRS also produced its own series of radio specials. The most widely regarded of these was *Command Performance*. Frank Sinatra became a regular and welcome guest on this latter presentation.

Most important of all for Sinatra, during his first year away from Dorsey, was to take over the coveted male-vocalist spot on *Your Hit Parade*, networked by CBS and sponsored by Lucky Strike Cigarettes. It was the most popular series of its kind, a forerunner of many future similar shows around the world.

During 1943, Sinatra commenced

Bob Hope and Frank Sinatra relaxing at a radio rehearsal.

his own series, *The Broadway Bandbox*, followed in 1944 by a short-lived series *The Frank Sinatra Program*, sponsored by Vimms. Like *Your Hit Parade*, both shows were networked by CBS. If you

hear them now, these programmes reveal Sinatra's marvellous consistency in performance. And Sinatra just got better and better on *Songs By Sinatra* (CBS, sponsored by Old Gold Cigarettes), which began in the fall of 1945 and continued until the end of 1947.

Sinatra's last major radio series of the Forties, ending in the spring of 1950, was *Light-Up Time*, sponsored again by Lucky Strike and networked by NBC. Although there was much to commend about his singing for most of the series' duration, there is no doubt that Sinatra's troubled times were starting to make inroads on The Voice itself during the last six months of the series.

Duets didn't start in the Nineties – of course not. Frank, on radio, with Dinah Shore.

GIGS

The reviews of Sinatra's earliest solo gigs all gave praise – some grudgingly – to the singer's night-club performances and his rarer appearances in concert. Even the Doubting Thomases were surprised not just at how well he sang, but also at the way he came across on stage. His deportment impressed the most hard-bitten critics; his timing and the way he used the stage (like other vocalists, he was more or less restricted to centre-stage due to the limitations imposed by stand-up microphones in use during the Forties) soon had audiences eating out of his hand.

Just how well Sinatra performed live can be gleaned from the faded cuttings of magazine and newspaper reviews: reactions tended to be ecstatic. And if perhaps you chance to meet up with someone who actually attended a gig some 50 years ago, they'll almost certainly confirm that Sinatra was most impressive.

Writing for a special "Sinatra-Is-Back" *Billboard* supplement in 1973, noted jazz critic/author/record producer Leonard Feather, remembered the first time he experienced one of Sinatra's solo performances. It was at the historic Riobamba Club engagement in 1943. Recalled the British-born Feather, "The smart, sophisticated night club crowd fixed its attention on the skinny youth as he approached the microphone. I sat at a not-far-from-the ringside table, watching him weave his head around in a gentle persuasive manner as he sang 'Embraceable You' and 'As Time Goes By'. It didn't take too much receptivity to notice particularly the combined effect of voice, delivery and personality on the feminine segment of the audience."

For a serious-minded performer such as Sinatra, reviews from critics such as Feather, George T. Simon and Dave Dexter Jr were more important than all the high-profile write-ups in the *New York Times* or the *Washington Post* put together. A good crit in either *Down Beat* or *Metronome* – publications for music *aficionados*, particularly lovers of jazz and swing – was eminently more satisfying to musicians and singers, especially since it would be read by their peers. Even though Sinatra seems always to have resented reviews that were not in the affirmative, music papers at least were more likely to provide a fair-minded representation of the way performers and bands played.

To assess at first hand just how excellent Sinatra actually sounded in live performance was almost impossible until recently. Just how superbly he could (and did) sing has now been demonstrated on numerous CD releases during the last ten years, especially *The Unheard Frank Sinatra/Radio Rarities 1943–1949, Volume 3*, which appeared several years ago. There are two extremely important examples of live Frank

The Forties Frank – year-by-year he was becoming a star performer – records, movies, concerts, on radio . . .

Sinatra on this recording, both from Hollywood Bowl concerts, dated August 1945 and August 1948, respectively.

The first comprises a five-song contribution Sinatra made to a special Academy Night Concert given in tribute to an ailing Jerome Kern. With Stordahl conducting his own arrangements and accompanied by a local symphony orchestra, Sinatra's quality of performance was astonishing. Starting with a wistful, beautifully-paced version of Kern's then popular "Long Ago And Far Away", he went on to sing a warm, gentle version of "I Should Care", which he'd recorded for Columbia five months before, and a deftly-phrased "What Makes The Sunset?", from his then current movie, *Anchors Aweigh!*.

Sinatra followed these up with an absolutely stunning interpretation of "If I Loved You" from the smash-hit Broadway production of *Carousel*. Of all the many versions – on record as well as live – he would perform over the years ahead, the Hollywood Bowl/1945 performance is the finest. Indeed, in the opinion of this writer, it might well be considered the the finest by any vocalist at any time.

To conclude his segment, Sinatra invested "Ol' Man River" with real authority and conviction. Like the previous number, this performance contained everything that made the singer a legend in his lifetime: the control is breathtaking, the diction and phrasing immaculate and deep feeling suffuses the entire reading. As you can hear today, the deep spell the singer wove was nearly broken a couple of times when some bobbysoxer squealed from the audience – but never quite; Sinatra quietly remonstrated with his young fans, in a firm, friendly and avuncular manner. His appearance at the same venue three years later was, once again, top-class Sinatra. Not quite as extraordinary, maybe, as 1945, but consistently brilliant nonetheless. This time the occasion was a Music For The Wounded charity.

Second time around, the programme was shorter. "Time After Time" had already passed into pop-music lore as Sinatra's personal property – and this was as fine a version as most others. "The Girl That I Marry" was similar to the Columbia recording of 1946 – full of charm, with the pauses-and-hesitations part of his technique quietly brought to bear. The finale was similar to 1945, except that on this occasion he chose the complete "Soliloquy" from *Carousel*. It was a stunning performance, which deftly removed – somehow – the basic schmaltz from this overblown opus and turned it into something else.

These days, serious admirers await with continued anticipation further fascinating insights into the live Sinatra of the Forties. In all probability, though, there aren't likely to be too many additions to the catalogue. After all, mobile tape-recordists were few-and-far-between in those days.

Oh that someone like the legendary Jerry Newman, who documented so much jazz magic of the Thirties, Forties and Fifties, had been prepared to lug his machine to at least one Sinatra gig in the post-Dorsey years …

Now hear this! Frank gives Judy Garland and her husband Sid Luft the gospel truth.

TELEVISION

Television was still in its infancy at the end of the Forties. Sinatra's own first involvement started on May 27, 1950, as a guest on *Star Spangled Review* (NBC). By October, he had been accorded his first regular series – *The Frank Sinatra Show* – which went out between October 1950 and June 1951. It was sponsored by Bulova and broadcast by CBS. Episodes were mostly an hour in duration, although some lasted 45 minutes. A follow-up series, this one sponsored by Echo, ran from October 1951 to April 1952. Regulars on both series were the ever-faithful Axel Stordahl plus his wife, singer June Hutton, together with her vocal group, the Hutton Tones.

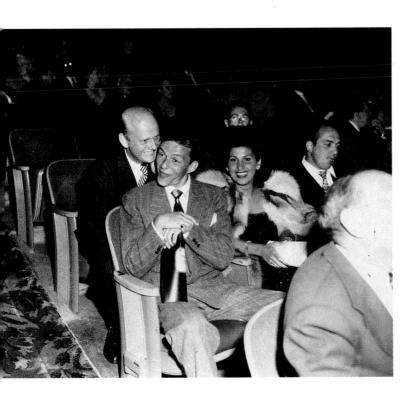

The series projected Frank Sinatra's talents in a pretty dull way visually. Viewed in retrospect, the settings and backdrops were of amateur-hour standard, the scripts not only dated but naive. Sinatra himself was sometimes clad in casual gear – check shirt and slacks, for example – in an apparent effort to present him in a more laid-back, accessible manner.

Perhaps because of professional and personal problems – especially an alarming throat-haemorrhage incident at the Copacabana – Sinatra's singing tended to vary. This condition could have been evidence of the strain from years of virtual non-stop performing.

However, there were occasions when any technical shortcomings were compensated for by a new, more basic kind of emotional delivery, for example on "You Are Love". And there were also intimations of a would-be swinger on "Get Happy". But for Frank Sinatra, full acceptance as a TV personality would have to wait until the latter half of the Fifties …

The Decline & Despair

The decline in the fortunes of Frank Sinatra during the late Forties and early Fifties was as dramatic as it was comprehensive. Failure touched nearly every area of his life.

Only Sinatra's most loyal fans stood by him as his professional reputation waned – slowly, at first, then accelerating at an alarming pace. Even the birth of his third child – Christine, in June 1948 – failed to lift the gathering gloom and wife Nancy was soon to file for separate maintenance.

Though he rarely sang poorly, the quality of Sinatra's early movies provided little scope for his acting ambitions: it hardly came as a shock when, at his own request, he was freed from his contract with MGM in April 1950.

Sinatra wasn't about to make a big comeback on TV either. A five-year CBS contract, guaranteeing him $250,000 a year, ended prematurely. Right from the opening broadcast on October 7, 1950, critics gave *The Frank Sinatra Show* a collective thumbs-down. A second series, premiered on October 9, 1951, foreclosed the following April, costing CBS a rumoured $1 million.

By September 1952, Sinatra had ended his 10-year association with Columbia Records still owing the company a reported $110,000 in unearned advances.

In December, the William Morris Agency took over from MCA as Sinatra's management company. MCA claimed he owed them $40,000 in back commissions – Sinatra said it was only $26,000. Just to rub salt into the gaping financial wound, the Internal Revenue presented the singer with a claim for $109,996 in back taxes.

On the gigs front, things were a little brighter. Sinatra may not have been pulling in the crowds like he used to but the applause – from critics and audiences alike – was still warm and genuine.

On one occasion, however, Sinatra experienced the ultimate singer's nightmare. At New York's Copacabana in March 1950, he was suffering from a throat ailment. Against doctor's advice, he came out for his third show in one evening. Suddenly, in mid-song, no sound came from his mouth. For several seconds, he was rooted to the spot looking terrified, then fled for the safety of his dressing room. Sinatra had suffered a sub-mucosal throat haemorrhage and this time acceded to his physician's request not to try to sing – or even talk – for at least two weeks.

Around this time, the Hit Parade was dominated by other male vocalists such as Johnny Ray, Guy Mitchell and Frankie Laine. Sinatra was also being outsold by the likes of Billy Eckstine, Perry Como and Nat King Cole. Between 1950 and 1952, he managed a trifling four Top 10 entries.

On top of all this, there was Ava Gardner, the voluptuous movie star from Grabtown, North Carolina, with whom Sinatra was totally infatuated: their doomed relationship had begun in the mid-Forties.

Ava Lavinia Gardner became the second Mrs Frank Sinatra in November 1951, a year after Nancy had secured an interlocutory decree of divorce.

Sinatra's courtship of Ava, and his attempts to keep their marriage intact, took a huge toll, physically, mentally and psychologically. Numerous close friends have said that, despite the all-too-frequent public rows and brawling, theirs was a genuine love affair ... although Ava's love, say many, turned to something approaching hatred.

The combination of a fast-fading career and troubled love life led Sinatra to despair, even, it has been alleged, to attempted suicide through drug overdose on August 31, 1951. Sinatra said it was just an allergic reaction to a small dose of sleeping tablets. Many years later, his long-time valet, George Jacobs, was sure his boss *did* try to take his life: it was only because he returned in the nick of time, that the singer survived ...

As 1951 ended, omens for the future looked bleak – if indeed there was to be a future. Very bleak indeed.

Two in love – wedding-day bliss for Ava and Frank. But their happiness was not destined to last.

The Golden Years

WHEN Sinatra finished reading James Jones' best-selling novel, *From Here To Eternity*, he was certain of one thing. He knew he was made for the part of the gutsy, ill-fated GI, Angelo Maggio, in the forthcoming movie from Columbia Pictures.

Sinatra: "Maggio for a grand" . . . Cohn: "You're a *singer!*"

The story of military life set in Schofield Barracks, Honolulu, around the time of Pearl Harbor, *From Here To Eternity* was full of dramatic action and ready-made for cinema. Motivated as much by the book's impressive early sales figures as by unanimous praise from the critics, Columbia Pictures' infamous studio chief, Harry Cohn, astutely snapped up the screen rights, decreeing that no expense be spared on this production and that only the biggest stars would do.

This was 1952 and Sinatra's career was on the skids: record sales were down; he owed thousands in back taxes to the IRS; his record label was dropping him; his agency was dropping him; his television and radio shows were dropping him. Things got so bad, Sinatra even started being nice to members of the press. Unfortunately, sections of the press didn't always reciprocate.

Looking for a lifeline, Sinatra came to believe that his own and Maggio's fates were intertwined – only the role of this fictitious Italian-American could save him from the vicious circle of gloom and despair. Since reading the novel, he had closely identified with the character,

"I knew Maggio. I went to school with him in Hoboken. I was beaten-up with him. I might have been Maggio ..."

Sinatra's reactionary opinion of modern pop was to soften considerably during the following decade – thanks largely to daughter Nancy's advice and success as a recording artist. This culminated in a massive Number 1 disc in 1966 – "These Boots Are Made For Walking" – and, the following year, another chart-topping triumph … this time in duet with her dad on "Somethin' Stupid"…

Along with many regular visits to Capitol's recording studios during the Fifties, Sinatra made numerous appearances on radio, culminating in the series *To Be Perfectly Frank*, containing his finest singing ever on the airwaves. Mid-1954 was also the start of an extraordinary increase in movie-making activity which meant that, during 1955, Sinatra was involved in no

Sinatra opens the new Ziegfeld Follies Winter Garden, NYC, in 1955. Gladys Gardner (far left) appeared in the 1915 edition of the original show, at age 15.

fewer than five major film productions. Towards the end of the decade, though, Sinatra's involvement with radio had all but ceased and it was during this period that he resumed his attempts to establish a reputation as a

major TV artist. The first series of *The Frank Sinatra Show* was transmitted in 1957.

Because of his increasing commitments to films and recording, Sinatra's availability for live performances became much more limited than his many admirers would have wished. Indeed, the majority might well have had to wait for years to see him on-stage, unless they could afford to visit Las Vegas for his appearances first at Caesar's Palace and then at the Sands Hotel.

Frank's first gigs at the Sands took place during the latter period of the "comeback" years. He was to play regular seasons there for the next 13 years. From the beginning, after obtaining the necessary gambling licence from the local Nevada state authority, he had invested $54,000 of his own money in the huge entertainment palace. Whether or not you could say that either the Caesar's Palace or Sands Hotel represent the Mecca of artistic inspiration, nevertheless, for the next three decades and more, these kind of venues were to become mainstays for Sinatra's live appearances.

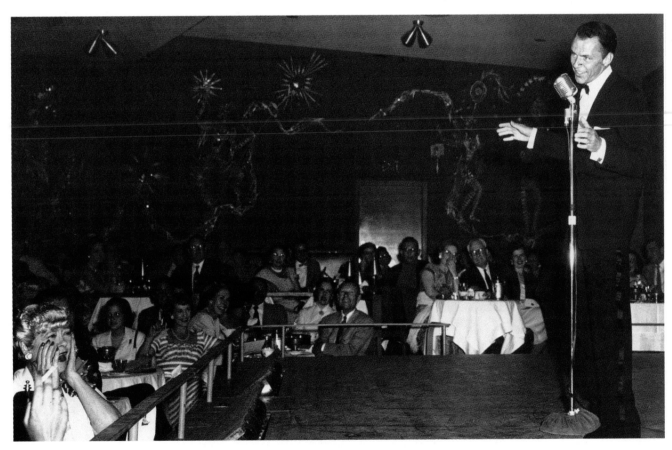

After the frenzied activity of the early Fifties, punters might have thought that the rest of the decade might find Sinatra easing off a bit, at least in his private life. No chance of that.

In July 1957, the divorce decree Ava Gardner had long sought was finally issued. In the same year, *Jazz* magazine chose Sinatra and Billie Holiday as joint Singers of the Year; Walter Winchell (*American Weekly*) called him the All-Round Entertainer of the Year; meanwhile *Metronome*'s Bill Coss said Sinatra was "the most complete, the most fantastic symbol of American maleness yet discovered".

Sinatra back at the Paramount in August 1956, backed by the band, led by Tommy (seen here) and Jimmy Dorsey.

Among the sad events of the latter half of the Fifties were the deaths of Sinatra's hero-buddy Bogart (1957, from throat cancer) and Manie Sachs (1958, heart attack). The death of

Tommy Dorsey, 51, was something which must have brought Sinatra's memories of the big-band days flooding back, temporarily, at least. The veteran bandleader had choked to death in his sleep on the night of November 26, 1956. Sadly, no one can recall messages of condolence from Sinatra. It would seem he had never forgiven Dorsey for giving him such a hard time when he left the band to embark on his solo career.

A promo shot for *A Hole In The Head*, or just Sinatra having fun in the photographic studio?

As the years went by, Sinatra's recording and movie making continued unabated; TV involvement picked up; and there was still time for regular live performances. There were to be further hit singles to complement increasingly successful albums – although nothing as classy as "All The Way", or the irresistible "Witchcraft" with its subtly-projected sexuality, or the equally compelling, finger-snapping "Nice 'N' Easy".

Sinatra connoisseurs had a point when they protested at the recording of novelty songs such as "French Foreign Legion" and a hip updating of "Ol' Macdonald". Despite the complaints, though, he sung (and swung) them both in joyous fashion ... and they were both hits.

There was also a run of so-so movies – *Some Came Running* (1958), *Never So Few* (1959) and *Ocean's Eleven* (1960) – involving members of the so-called Clan (Dean Martin, Peter Lawford, Shirley MacLaine, Joey Bishop and Sammy Davis Jr), a group of self-indulgent friends, whose outrageous social life had begun to take up reams of space in newspapers and magazines. The antics of the Clan all too often bordered on the infantile and included, for example, barging-in on a legit live performance by Eddie Fisher, and a virtual take-over of the show.

At first, the media were amused. Then, faint amusement turned into a gathering tirade against Sinatra & Co. One columnist, in comparing the group to Humphrey Bogart's near-legendary Holmby Hills Rat Pack – of which Sinatra was actually a member – declared that at least its predecessor kept its collective doings reasonably private: the Clan preferred to go public with its flamboyant antics. Sinatra's riposte was, simply, that the Clan was "a figment of someone's imagination". In fact, he added, they were merely a group of friends who met to enjoy each other's company.

Swingin' Lovers remains many peoples' Number 1 all-time favourite album – since its first release in the UK in 1956, it has in all probability never been absent from the Capitol catalogue. There are those, however, who believe that it is possibly inferior to its successor, *A Swingin' Affair*. The 15 rhythmic tracks here comprise an interesting repertoire, including Ellington's "I Got It Bad", and "From This Moment On", "Night And Day" (Sinatra's third recording) and the often underrated "At Long Last Love", all from the pen of Cole Porter. As appealing as are the majority of the "swingin'" albums, one has to search through the ballad collections for the definitive Frank Sinatra, such as *Close To You*, or *In The Wee Small Hours*, or *Only The Lonely* – each masterminded with keen attention to detail by Nelson Riddle.

But the two Jenkins sets also touched the heights. *Where Are You?* makes for absorbing listening, at anytime; year by year, it seems to become more meaningful, more vital. Once again, there is not a weak link in this skilful chain of emotional singing-arranging-playing. Perhaps the recapitulation of "I'm A Fool To Want You" lacks the rawness of the Columbia version, but it is a masterpiece nevertheless. The most memorable track of all is a reading of "Autumn Leaves", which is like no other. Haunting, yes; emotive, certainly. But even more than these qualities, Sinatra's unfolding of Johnny Mercer's English lyric produces an aura of mystery that at times borders on the surreal.

Not only does this moving version of "Autumn Leaves" rank with the singer's most compelling performances on record. It is so extraordinary, there is absolutely no chance of anyone else equalling, let alone surpassing, it.

In The Wee Small Hours has been the musicians' choice since it first appeared in 1955. Each of the songs seems to have been hand-picked. Some, like the exquisitely-phrased "Dancing On The Ceiling", "I'll Be Around" (with its supreme control) and "Glad To Be Unhappy" (Sinatra here matching cynicism with his own brand of home-spun philosophy) have accompaniments provided by a simple four- or five-piece rhythm section. Elsewhere, Riddle has

A stylish, relaxed Sinatra, character-istics of his output during the Captiol years.

furnished inspiring, but never intrusive, definitely superior backgrounds. It seems almost churlish to select further highlights from the rest, but Sinatra's interpretations of "Deep In A Dream", "In The Wee Small Hours Of The Morning", "I Get Along Without You Very Well" and, finest of all the 15 cuts, a magisterial "Last Night When We Were Young" – the final word, surely, on Harold Arlen's magnum opus – are matchless.

Three years on, *Only The Lonely* (1958) was, if anything, more emotional than *In The Wee Small Hours*. The voice is coarser, certainly; but this adds even more depth to the interpretation. And Nelson Riddle never wrote more feelingly. "Spring Is Here", "Willow, Weep For Me", "Blues In The Night", "What's New?" and "Gone With The Wind" – thanks to the combined efforts of Sinatra and Riddle, each one sounded like a brand-new number. The sadly-neglected "It's A Lonesome Old Town" simply defines loneliness, with no high-flown drama; both "Angel Eyes" and "One For My Baby" are the finest of Sinatra's favourite saloon-song performances.

Songs For Young Lovers and *Come Fly With Me* represent the finest of the eclectic albums. The latter benefits from Billy May's first charts for Sinatra. Their coming-together produced a series of flamboyant performances, epitomized by the Cahn-Van Heusen title tune, plus an hilarious re-creation of Kipling's "(On The) Road To Mandalay", as well as uplifting collaborations on "Let's Get Away From It All" and "It's Nice To Go Trav'ling" (more new Cahn-Van Heusen). The irresistibility of the swingers is complemented by a series of superior ballad selections. "London By Night" and "Autumn In New York" are merely excellent; "April In Paris" and "Moonlight In Vermont" are near-flawless … even by Sinatra's greatest balladeering standards.

Young Lovers is even more of an all-round masterpiece than *Come Fly With Me*. Each of its eight titles sees Sinatra at his peak. The swingers – scored expertly by George Siravo – find the singer as close to jazz as anywhere on record, with "A Foggy Day" and "I Get A Kick Out Of You" at the top of the pile; the same goes for the Riddle-arranged ballads, "My Funny Valentine", "Like Someone In Love", " The Girl Next Door", and "Violets For Your Furs". Such was Sinatra's omnipotence during the Fifties that even collections comprising single releases or out-cuts, such as *This Is Sinatra*, *This Is Sinatra, Volume Two* and *Look To Your Heart* – [All on *This Is Frank Sinatra 1953–1957*] – tend to sound like single-album productions in their own right.

Ultimately, though, it was to be Sinatra's thematic albums which were to pass into pop-music lore.

MOVIES

EVEN NOW, it's hard to say whether it was movies or recordings which played the bigger part in reviving Frank Sinatra's career in the period following *From Here To Eternity*.

Certainly, there's no doubt that Sinatra's re-emergence as a movie star helped him immeasurably in becoming the biggest name in show business, especially since he was now considered a "serious" actor of real stature. Indeed, many of the fans who materialized during the Fifties – the most significant decade of Sinatra's career – were first drawn by his appearances on the silver screen and only later became interested in the man's music.

Sinatra's Maggio in *From Here To Eternity* captured the imaginations of committed cinema-goers as well as casual film fans, and the impact of the Academy Award which followed reverberated throughout Hollywood and the entertainment industry. Sinatra's period in the doldrums was over – suddenly he was able to pick and choose what work he wanted ... even though Maggio would remain, forever, his movie milestone.

Even before the applause had died away, Sinatra had taken on a leading role in *Suddenly* (1954), portraying a sadistic, would-be

Left: As Frankie Machine in *The Man With The Golden Arm*.

Background: With Edward G. Robinson in *A Hole in The Head*.

Presidential assassin with a conviction that riveted the attention ... as with *Eternity*, he was still obviously in debt to Monty Clift. Critical acclaim for this role proved that Sinatra's acting in *Eternity* had been no fluke.

From this point on, Sinatra's career in motion pictures was on the up. True, there was at least one real disaster – *Johnny Concho* (1956), a brave attempt to make the main character in a Western (played by first-time producer Sinatra) an out-and-out coward – but, for the most part, Sinatra's films continued to triumph.

The heady mixture of nine major movies that followed *Eternity* included dramatic parts for Sinatra in all manner of non-singing productions, out-and-out musicals, films which called for both acting and singing, plus comedy within a musical context.

Throughout, Sinatra continued to demonstrate top-grade acting, most notably as a heroin-addicted card dealer in *The Man With The Golden Arm* (1955) and, two years later, with his portrayal of alcoholic night-club comedian, Joe E. Lewis, in *The Joker Is Wild*.

Sinatra's stand-out performance as Frankie Machine in an otherwise disappointing *Golden Arm* hit the mark perfectly. The high spot was a lengthy scene with Machine alone in a locked bedroom, trying to kick his long-time drug habit. Apparently, its realistic quality stemmed from a period the actor spent closely observing junkies' withdrawal symptoms in a controlled hospital situation. A second Oscar nomination came as no surprise but ultimately the award for Best Actor went to Ernest Borgnine.

1957 was the year in which Sinatra completed three full-length movies, so it came as a shock when he failed to receive a single nomination at the relevant Academy Awards, especially for his acting-singing contributions to *The Joker Is Wild*. Still, Sinatra must have been pleased that his song writing buddies, Sammy Cahn and Jimmy Van Heusen, copped Best Song honours for "All The Way", the picture's "big" number.

Pal Frankie – Book-ended, but not bewitched, by Hayworth and Novak.

The star could also console himself with the fact that it was his acting which dominated a fine, atmospheric production. As for the soundtrack, apart from a first-time version of "All The Way", Sinatra's performances of standards such as "I Cried For You" and "If I Could Be With You One Hour Tonight" are less than totally successful. Although jazz-based vocals provided an appropriate "period" feel and style, his attempts at swinging in 2/4 simply weren't convincing – with the exception of "Chicago". The truth is

Sinatra has always been a 4/4 performer ...

Pal Joey (1957), predictably, presented no such problems for Sinatra. Showing a fine comedic talent witnessed previously in *The Tender Trap* (also 1957), he was in peak vocal form taking on an all-Rodgers and Hart score.

"The Lady Is A Tramp" – Sinatra's most exhilarating musical performance.

Sadly, apart from songs such as "Bewitched" and "I Could Write A Book", this wasn't the score from the original Broadway smash-hit production. Gone were several delightful numbers, including some of Hart's most witty and inventive lyrics – e.g. "Take Him"; "Happy Hunting Horn"; "In Our Little Den Of Iniquity" – while other gems – "You Mustn't Kick It Around"; "Plant You Now, Dig You Later"; "Do It The Hard Way" – were relegated to mere background music for on-screen club sequences.

For the dedicated Sinatra fan, however, there is much to savour. His elegant readings of "Bewitched" and "I Could Write A Book", from the stage version, and "I Didn't Know What Time It Was", as well as "There's A Small Hotel" (from two other R&H Broadway musicals) were well up to par, and this screen version of "The Lady Is A Tramp", yet another import, produced a truly electrifying performance.

The scene where Sinatra "serenades" Rita Hayworth in an after-hours performance at a night-club remains, forever, his single most exhilarating musical performance of all his 25 motion-picture appearances containing any kind of musical content.

The remainder of Sinatra's film work in the Fifties was an interesting mixture to say the least. There were a couple of other strong non-musical productions – *Not As A Stranger* (1955), with Sinatra shaping up to strong acting competition from Robert Mitchum, Broderick Crawford and Charles Bickford, and *A Hole In The Head* (1959), with Edward G. Robinson heading an even more impressive cast that included the likes of Thelma Ritter, Eleanor Parker, Keenan Wynn and Carolyn Jones. This production also featured the Oscar-winning "High Hopes" as well as the dreadfully underrated "All My Tomorrows", sung beautifully off-screen, over the credits, by Sinatra.

Both *High Society* (1956) and *Young At Heart* (1955) contained more fine vocals. The former featured Sinatra's debut

TELEVISION

IT TOOK Frank Sinatra much longer than most of his contemporaries to establish himself as a contributor to the medium of television.

Other than the odd guest-spot, his initial involvement came during the "dark days" between 1950 and 1951 with the first-ever *Frank Sinatra Show*. The series was less than an overwhelming success and somehow its host never really looked the part on the small screen – the beginning of the Fifties wasn't exactly peak Sinatra in terms of vocal projection.

After *From Here To Eternity*, Sinatra plunged into hectic movie-making and record-making; any spare time he had was set aside for gigs. Of course, there were rare appearances on TV but, by the mid-Fifties, Sinatra had become unenthusiastic about this fastest-growing section of the media. Indeed, he was known to sound off against it in no uncertain terms.

In 1955, Sinatra told A E Hotchner, of the Canadian *Redbook* magazine, "Man, I've seen (TV) chew up a lot of talent from a lot of great people. Let's face it, I'm not fond of TV. It takes too much energy, too much tension, havoc and rehearsals for the results you get. I know what it can do to your inside. I had a one-hour weekly show for CBS for a whole year. The only guy I know who has survived and made it pay is Ed Sullivan – the modern Rudy Vallee. Ed is making profit out of 1905 vaudeville! Show him Fink's mules and he'll grab 'em and put 'em out there ..."

But Sinatra reserved his most caustic comments for the people who ran US television, "My blood boils when I see the mediocrities who are sitting at the top of the TV networks; refugees from ad agencies who think that show business is stuck together with spit and gimmicks ... In TV, mediocrities have inherited the earth."

It took until 1957 before a brand new *Frank Sinatra Show* was unveiled again. Indeed, the show business world pricked up its ears when the ABC network announced that Frank Sinatra had signed a three-year contract to star in his own TV specials – the original plan was for 13 half-hour musical and 13 half-hour drama productions. The series began on October 18 and included two live hour-long specials with Chesterfield Cigarettes as sponsors. For his not inconsiderable services, the star performer received a cheque for a cool $3 million.

However, the critics didn't exactly rave about the opening show, which had guest spots for Bob Hope, Peggy Lee and Kim Novak. There were no complaints about the host's singing – hard-swinging performances of "The Lonesome Road", "I Get A Kick Out Of You" and 'The Lady Is A Tramp"; superior ballad-singing on "I Could Write A Book", 'All The Way", "Bewitched" and a touching "Autumn Leaves". The criticisms were about the show itself and its general concept. "Banal", shouted one reviewer, while another felt the attempts at humour were less than successful.

It wasn't a happy augury for the future. By November, ratings had dipped. But the show survived until the following May. By this time, Chesterfield had withdrawn sponsorship and the final three transmissions came courtesy of Bulova. Watched years later, the dialogue sounds contrived, the humour forced; the non-musical sections were at best throwaway additions. On the positive side, the guest roster was usually up to the mark. Visiting vocalists included Dinah Shore, Keely Smith, Ethel Merman, Ella Fitzgerald, Jo Stafford, Bing Crosby and Rat Pack buddies, Dean Martin and Sammy Davis Jr.

Rehearsin's so cool. While Frank takes his ease, Dino goes for a shoe-shine.

Noel Coward introduced the special guest in glowing terms – both in French and English, "Never once a breach of taste, never once a wrong note". And an obviously buoyant Sinatra treated the glitter-and-gold audience to 40 minutes of superb singing, plus some typical "rest-period" chat. "I've Got You Under My Skin" was projected in an even more overtly sexual way than usual ("We may all get arrested tonight!" he interpolated at one stage), and "Come Fly With Me" soared triumphantly. "Where Or When", sung mostly with just piano accompaniment, which he would record for Capitol in the same format, got a breathtaking treatment; and both "Moonlight In Vermont" and "April In Paris" were executed with supreme assurance – the hangover phrases were carried through effortlessly.

But for many of the audience, Sinatra's idiosyncratic "(On The) Road To Mandalay" probably registered strongest. In terms of topicality, "Monique", a song inspired by *Kings Go Forth*, received its debut live performance – the Midnight Gala took place after the premiere of the movie [*Sinatra: Monte Carlo 14 June 1958*]. As exceptional as any of the concerts mentioned above was that which took place on April 1, 1959 at the West Melbourne Stadium in Australia – [*Frank Sinatra With The Red Norvo Quintet Live In Australia 1959*]. The freewheeling Sinatra who thrilled the Aussies was accompanied by a five-man combo, fronted by vibist Red Norvo. From a spring-heeled opening "I Could Have Danced All Night", right through to as dynamic a "Night And Day" as he can ever have performed live, Sinatra was at his most electrifying. Altogether, 50 minutes of Sinatra magic …

In terms of flawless singing, from start to finish, those fortunate enough to be present at a Sinatra appearance at the 500 Club, Atlantic City [*The Sinatra Saga*], still rave, years later. Opening with a whirlwind "Too Marvellous For Words", his performance, as one member of the audience remembers, "was like no other in-person appearance I can recall. There were times, I swear, when he seemed like a guy possessed. He did 'I Could Have Danced All Night' – we all were sure he could've sung all night!"

Jim Biddulph, a retired businessman from Philadelphia, is sure that "there were versions of several of the tunes – 'Too Marvellous' was one, 'Moonlight In Vermont' and 'All the Way' were others – that he just cannot have sung better. At anytime …"

Doing it *his* way? Sinatra in charge at rehearsals, telling the guys what he needs at showtime.

The Reprise Years

"To play & play again"...
but not forever?

LEGEND HAS IT that in December 1960 Frank Sinatra passed by the new and impressive Capitol Tower building in Hollywood with record company executive, Mo Ostin. He turned to Ostin and said,

"I helped to build that. Now, let's build one of my own."

The following year, the dream of running his own record label had become reality. And throughout the Sixties, though there was to be no let-up in Sinatra's movie-making and television activities, it was primarily Reprise Records which would continue to keep its founder and first boss in the spotlight.

From the outset, Sinatra was determined to build up a strong roster of talent. During 1962, Reprise's first year in business, Sammy Davis Jr, Dean Martin, Jimmy Witherspoon and Sinatra's eldest daughter, Nancy then aged 20, were among those who became affiliated to the new label. Soon Bing Crosby, Count Basie and Nelson Riddle were to sign up too.

Sinatra on Reprise – some disappointments maybe, but his recordings for the label did not lack variety.

Sinatra offered his artists the kind of arrangement he himself had sought from Capitol: each of them was to retain ownership of their recording masters; they would organize their own sessions; and there were no restrictions on their involvement with other record companies.

For Frank Sinatra and many of his contemporaries, the Sixties proved frustrating. Record companies, large and small, were concentrating their efforts on catering to the youth market, which was growing at an astounding rate. Non-rock artists came under pressure to conform.

However, apart from the single "Everybody's Twistin'", Sinatra maintained an unswerving indifference to changing styles. At first, the Reprise label had virtually no hits in the singles market, but something had to give.

Thanks to Sammy Davis Jr, a breakthrough occurred in late 1962 with "What Kind Of Fool Am I?", which got into the Top 20. Then came a Top Five for Reprise, also in 1962, with comedian Lou Monte's less-than-scintillating "Pepino – The Italian Mouse". Exactly a year later, a young Texan, Trini Lopez, became the highest-placed Reprise artist so far, when "If I Had A Hammer" rocketed to No 3. It was Dean Martin, though, who really put Reprise on the map with "Everybody Loves Somebody" – an old Sinatra song! – which went to the top of the US Hit Parade.

Survival was ensured late in 1963, when Warner's chief, Jack L Warner, agreed to purchase two-thirds of Reprise Records. The deal brought Sinatra Enterprises under the Warner umbrella with one-third of Warner Bros Records falling into Sinatra's possession.

Four years later, Sinatra sold a further 13 percent of Reprise to Warner-Seven Arts for $4,200,000; the remaining 20 percent he sold to Kinney National Service, which itself would eventually take over Warner-Seven Arts (in March, 1969) for a further $22,500,000 in cash and convertible debentures. In total, it is estimated, Sinatra received around $80 million for his record company.

In order that the newly-created Reprise division of Warner Bros. Records should start making real money, its 1961-63 roster was drastically pruned. Former MGM, now Reprise, executive Mo Ostin initiated the signing of new artists, with the emphasis this time placed on an ever-broadening rock horizon.

Even more ambitious, perhaps, was Warners' view that Sinatra, Martin and other older-generation artists could make their mark in the rock and pop market – as part of a "soft-rock" division. With a view to bringing them back into the singles charts, newcomers producer Jimmy Bowen and arranger Ernie Freeman were assigned to work on both Martin and Sinatra.

Freeman in particular took a lot of stick from critics for the kind of pop charts he produced for Sinatra. Nonetheless, the very first Sinatra-Freeman-Bowen collaboration produced a beautifully-felt version of "Softly, As I Leave You", with big-band brass-reeds, plus strings, with classic rock triplets in the chart and drummer Hal Blaine laying down a basic beat in prescribed soft-rock style.

Success in re-establishing Frank Sinatra as a major pop singer took rather longer than had been imagined. The song that wrought the change – and what a change! – in Sinatra's fortunes was a tune by German band leader Bert Kaempfert, with English lyrics by Charles Singleton and Eddie Snyder.

A good, if by no means outstanding, performance by Sinatra of an ordinary number, "Strangers In The Night" received massive airplay on all but the heaviest rock stations in the States. In practically no time, it was topping the charts in the US and the UK. It went on to make the Number 1 position in four other territories around the world. In fact, it was the biggest single hit Frank Sinatra would ever achieve – bigger than anything from the Columbia or Capitol eras.

For Sinatra, it was not just an important breakthrough. It opened the flood-gates. Back-catalogue album material took on a new life. And the new album – predictably entitled *Strangers In The Night* – sold prodigiously, even though it scarcely ranked as an artistic masterpiece. Still, not only was it the biggest-selling Sinatra LP on Reprise, it was his first chart-topper since *Nice'N'Easy* in 1960. And there was a further hit single during 1966, the gutsy, R&B-based "That's Life". As if that wasn't enough, during this halcyon period, Frank, duetting with daughter Nancy, saw "Somethin' Stupid" become a mega-hit in 1967.

A couple of years on, the song destined to become the Sinatra anthem was released. Of French origin and titled "Comme d'Habitude", it was written by Jacques Revaux, Claude François and Gilles Thibout. In 1967, former teenage pop idol Paul Anka,

By the Sixties, Sinatra live was second to none – *the* consummate vocal performer.

penned English lyrics and "My Way", retitled and published by Anka, rapidly became a modern standard (covered by, among others, Elvis Presley, Dorothy Squires and even Sid Vicious, plus Anka himself).

Curiously, "My Way" was never a massive hit for Sinatra in the US, but it achieved extraordinary popularity among British record-buyers. Whereas it just squeezed into the Top 30 in Sinatra's own country, its chart longevity in the UK was astounding. Following its initial entry on 2 April 1969, it remained in the charts, on and off, for nearly three years. *Nine* chart entries in all. No other record – by any other artist, at any time – has ever made such an impact on a singles chart.

On the personal front, there were several events during the Sixties which caused Sinatra genuine grief and deep-down pain. The assassinations of the Kennedy brothers and Martin Luther King hit him badly. In particular, he rated Jack Kennedy as a personal friend – even though his aspirations to become a regular White House visitor never materialized.

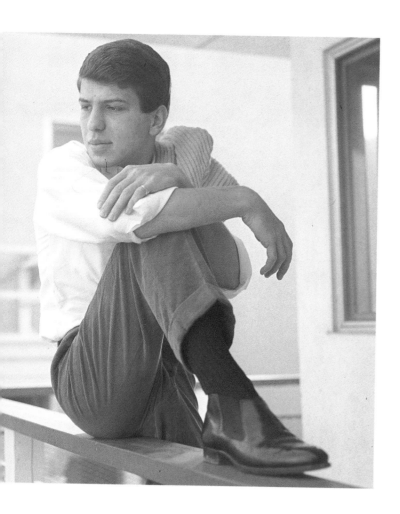

The kidnap of Frank Jr brought his father close to despair.

Sinatra was also shaken to the core by the death of his father, at the age of 74 from a combination of a major heart condition and emphysema. Those close to Sinatra insisted they'd never seen him as emotionally distraught. Other deaths that caused him distress during the decade were those of Marilyn Monroe, Spencer Tracy and his former press agent, Mark Millar.

The omens for 1963 were good, but pride and delight would soon be followed by shock and near-despair.

Frank Sinatra Jr made an unbilled debut appearance with the resident orchestra at Disneyland in 1962 and gigs which followed included a season at the plush Royal Box of Manhattan's Americana Hotel in September 1963. To Sinatra's delight, Junior's reviews were mostly favourable. Three months later came the event which caused such distress to his father, family and friends.

Junior was appearing in Vegas, again, this time at the Harrah's Lake Tahoe Casino. On Sunday 8 December, he and a colleague were dining in Sinatra's motel room, prior to the first show of the evening. Pretending to be room service, two men gained entry to the premises. One threatened the pair with a revolver. His accomplice bound and gagged Sinatra's colleague, while the young singer was blindfolded, then forced into a waiting car. Frank Jr had been kidnapped.

Almost a day after the abduction, Sinatra Sr received a phone call to say that Junior was alive. On instruction, Sinatra drove to Carson City and a ransom sum was mentioned. Eventually, he was told to wait at Nancy's residence, in Bel-Air.

Next, Sinatra was ordered to leave $240,000, in cash inside a telephone booth at Los Angeles Airport. From there, he was redirected to a service station outside LA, then, to a Texaco station in a completely different direction. Finally, he was told to leave the case full of dough in between two parked school buses. Sinatra didn't deposit the cash – this task was performed by an FBI agent. By this time, it was Wednesday ...

A call to Nancy stated that Junior would be released at an overpass at the Mulholland and San Diego Freeway. Dad left in great haste, by car, accompanied by Federal agents. They returned just over 30 minutes later – alone. Shortly afterwards, a private policeman, driving in Bel-Air, was hailed by a young man, with a blindfold hanging limply around his neck. He recognized Frank Sinatra Jr. The young man and his family were reunited at three the following morning. Father's 48th birthday, the next day, turned out to be rather more of a celebration than had been planned.

(By Saturday, the FBI had arrested three men. Each was bailed at $50,000. After trial at the US District Court of Los Angeles, the following March, two of the kidnappers received life imprisonment, plus 75 years; the third received a lesser sentence – he'd been kind to Junior – of 16 years, eight months.)

Sinatra Sr found himself in real danger the following February. During the shooting of *None But The Brave*, a World War II pic, on Kauai, one of a small group of Hawaiian islands, he narrowly escaped drowning. While bathing offshore, he was engulfed by a huge wave at Wailua Bay and was soon in serious trouble.

Brad Dexter, an experienced film actor – and member of the cast – dived into the surf after Sinatra. A strong swimmer, Dexter just got to the fast-fading star, who by this time was suffering from hypoxia.

Sinatra's gratitude to Dexter was shown by the latter's immediate acceptance into the exclusive small-knit community of Frank's friends. He also gave Dexter a substantial part in his next movie, *Von Ryan's Express*. And Dexter's debut as screen producer came under Sinatra's auspices, two years later (1967), with *The Naked Runner*. It was the last occasion the pair would work together. Friendship between them ended when Dexter, it has been reported, said he could no longer take Sinatra's temperamental outbursts.

Frank Sinatra's marriage to the *gamine* Mia Farrow provided one of the gossip-columnists' favourite leads - even months before the actual event, which took place on 19 July 1966. Once again, as romance developed, the cynics sharpened their knives. After all, wasn't she a slim-line 19 when the couple first met (on the set of *Von Ryan's Express*) and wasn't he almost 50? Despite the general thumbs-down from those in the know, the pair grew fonder of each other as the months passed by.

The wedding ceremony took place at the Sands Hotel. The hotel's boss, Jack Entratter, acted as one of the witnesses before the couple left for their honeymoon in New York, London and Cap d'Antibes. Despite continued pessimism in some quarters, the marriage began to take shape. But the liaison lasted only 16 months.

It was Sinatra who started divorce proceedings. His wife was heartbroken. Ultimately, though, he persuaded Mia to seek a quick divorce.

A tense moment for Sinatra in *The Naked Runner*.

This, she did – with great reluctance – in Juarez, Mexico. The date: 16 August 1968.

Throughout the Sixties, Sinatra kept falling out with people. Another break-up of a personal (and business) relationship had occurred in 1963. This was the split between Frank and his long-time buddy and business associate Hank Sanicola, just after the former had had his gaming licence revoked by the Nevada Gaming Board. The pair rowed and Sinatra rarely spoke to Sanicola again.

Charisma,
communication, class:
Sinatra displayed all
these characteristics in
the Sixties, in concert,
on disc and on
television.

Sinatra's fourth album for his own label was all-ballad, and *Sinatra & Strings* remains one of his finest albums. There is a passion and intensity – complemented, at times, with tenderness – that gives each performance a compelling quality. A rough edge to the voice gives added depth to such items as "I Hadn't Anyone Till You", "Don't Take Your Love From Me" and "Prisoner Of Love". "Night And Day", for so long associated with Sinatra, received its most expressive reading ever – the delivery of the verse is pure musical onomatopoeia.

The arrangements on *Sinatra & Strings* rank with any comparable backgrounds he worked with. These were the creations of Boston-born Don Costa (1915–1986), the third newcomer to the growing list of Sinatra's writers in the early Sixties.

Arranger Gordon Jenkins was recalled for Album Number Five, which was also string based. But *All Alone* failed to hit the mark, mainly because of its poor choice of repertoire. There was one superb piece of Sinatra-Jenkins, an achingly sad version of Irving Berlin's autobiographical "When I Lost You".

Further movement among Sinatra's arrangers found Neal Hefti scoring *Sinatra & Swingin' Brass*, which was, if anything, more jazz-oriented than *Ring-a-Ding Ding!* This time, there was a total absence of strings. And Hefti's charts never failed to swing, though the album is maybe a little busy in places (viz. "Pick Yourself Up", with its contrapuntal passages).

For the most part, there is much to appreciate in the singing, especially on "Don'cha Go 'Way Mad", (Porter's) "I Love You", "Tangerine", "I'm Beginning To See The Light" and "Serenade In Blue" (the sole ballad).

Writer Number Seven, Robert Farnon, wielded the baton to his own string-based arrangements as Musical Director for the overall-disappointing *Great Songs From Great Britain*.

There was much *brouhaha* from Reprise's HQ in breaking the news that Frank Sinatra would be making his first-ever recordings with the Count Basie Orchestra. After all, a meeting between the Chairman of the Board (as WNEW disc jockey William B Williams had dubbed Sinatra) and the legendary jazz big band represented a summit meeting of two giant talents of the music world.

The resultant album – *Sinatra-Basie* – never fully lived up to its billing. On the positive side, the Rolls-Royce of post-war jazz orchestras provided the most lasting moment of *Sinatra-Basie* – a glorious, utterly inimitable, chorus on "I Won't Dance". Sinatra ("I've waited 20 years for this ...") was, understandably, in awe of the band. It shows, too, for most of the album. He rarely sounded relaxed and the necessity of being locked into the band's fundamental 4/4 time signature seems to have been a problem.

A follow up studio collaboration didn't materialize until two-and-a-half years later. It was even less successful than the first. For one thing, *It Might As Well Be Swing* was a misleading description of the album's contents. Quincy Jones was in charge of arrangements and, frankly, they do not rank with that great man's finest. However, in two selections – "Fly Me To The Moon" and "The Best Is Yet To Come" – Sinatra, Jones and the band coalesce splendidly and show what might have been. They are the only memorable fruits of a thoroughly disappointing venture.

During the second half of the Sixties, Frank Sinatra and Count Basie worked together live on a fairly regular basis. Their third – and final – get-together on vinyl was the recording of a live performance for *Sinatra At The Sands*. Taped over several nights of their joint appearance at the Sands Hotel between 26 January and 1 February 1966, it was not only the best of their on-record collaborations, but represented the first time that Sinatra would release a live album – a two-LP set.

Sinatra's next studio album was a long-overdue reunion with arranger Nelson Riddle – except for a couple of singles dates, the first time they'd worked together for Reprise.

Perhaps, though, the concept of *The Concert Sinatra* was rather overblown. After all, did Sinatra really need Riddle to conduct an orchestra of over 60 pieces? Nevertheless, the results of this new undertaking were mostly fine. Only "Lost In The Stars" drew a less-than-convincing reading from the singer. Elsewhere, there were full-blooded versions of "Ol' Man River", "You'll Never Walk Alone" and "This Nearly Was Mine", plus an impassioned, superbly sustained "Soliloquy" from *Carousel*. Even better, though, were first-time recordings of "I Have Dreamed" and "My Heart Stood Still".

Sinatra in the studio, early-Sixties: with Robert Farnon (facing page, top and bottom right); Basie (bottom left) and the Basie band (background image).

Nelson Riddle also worked on *Sinatra's Sinatra*, which comprised reworkings of eleven Sinatra standards. The album offered evidence that perhaps it's best to leave the past to the past: not one of the new versions can be said to offer an improvement on previous recordings. Riddle's last truly superb charts for entire Sinatra albums came with *Days Of Wine And Roses* (1964) and *Moonlight Sinatra* (1965). On the former set, the quartet of rhythm numbers easily came off best. Sinatra's timing on Crosby's "Swinging On A Star" was perfect. "The Way You Look Tonight", "In The Cool, Cool, Cool Of The Evening", "Days Of Wine And Roses" and "The Continental" were also successes. The ballads were not altogether well chosen, however. Both "It Might As Well Be Spring" and "Three Coins In The Fountain" were, like the new "Moon River", acceptable; but "Secret Love" remained very much the property of Doris Day; and "Love Is A Many-Splendored Thing" was, ultimately, The Four Aces', not Sinatra's. The all-ballad *Moonlight Sinatra* proved average-only fare. The final Sinatra/Riddle collaboration of the decade, *Strangers In The Night*, was a rush-job, a hotch-potch collection of oldies and newer things. Sinatra's reluctance to be hustled into the studio for a new album is shown by the unconvincing vocals on "My Baby Just Cares For Me", "You're Driving Me Crazy", "Call Me" and "Downtown". The only track that deserves any kind of praise was "Summer Wind", a superior Johnny Mercer ballad with a lilting swing.

After years of trying, Warners finally succeeded in their efforts to hoist Sinatra's name high among the biggest-selling rock artists. But, along the way, Sinatra was given an abundance of wretched material to record. *Cycles*, the album, was in many ways typical of the hotch-potch collections that were released during the mid-Sixties.

Its delightful, folksy title tune became a modest hit in the US. "Little Green Apples", a charming if perhaps naive-sounding Bobby Russell piece, likewise made *Cycles* a better-than-average "modern" Sinatra album. The pièce de resistance here, though, was the finest of all the numerous recordings of "By The Time I Get To Phoenix". Phrasing in classic style and sublime in his lyric-reading, Sinatra gave an undramatic, yet deeply-felt interpretation which the Jim Webb masterpiece would never receive elsewhere.

Don Costa produced a series of beautifully-sculpted charts for *A Man Alone* (1968), the album of Rod McKuen songs (and poems). And it was mostly the quiet understatement, vocally and instrumentally, which raised *A Man Alone* to a status of a real classic-ballad Sinatra collection, epitomized by individual tracks such as "Lonesome Cities", "I've Been To Town", "A Man Alone" and the wry "Love's Been Good To Me" (a major hit single in the UK).

Don Costa's arranging talents also contributed to *My Way*. As an album, it remains indicative of the erratic quality of some of Sinatra's offerings during this period. Worst of all was the brutal treatment meted out to Paul Simon's subtle and gentle "Mrs Robinson". Sadly, Costa takes a large share of the blame, with a sledgehammer arrangement that endeavoured to be a kind of big-band-Basie bash. Sinatra has a ball, it's true, but at the expense of the humour and content of the song's lyric. His substitution of "Jilly" for "Jesus" and the addition of "Keep those cards and letters comin' in, baby!" as a spoken coda were both tasteless and inappropriate.

The two Sinatra albums of the latter half of the Sixties that have rightly been acknowledged as masterpieces were the autobiographical *September Of My Years* (1965) and *Francis Albert Sinatra & Antonio Carlos Jobim* (1969). Those who worked closely with Sinatra on the first-named have spoken with real pride of their involvement in the project. A project which dealt – unashamedly, tenderly, wistfully and sometimes humorously – with the subject of impending middle age. For Sinatra, it was the right time to make such a recorded statement – after all, he would be celebrating his 50th birthday at the year's end.

Sinatra himself was elated at the results. He must have known, for instance, that his reworkings of "Hello, Young Lovers" and "September Song" were considerable improvements on all previous versions. Even if, technically speaking, "Last Night When We Were Young" could not hope to surpass the recording on Capitol, it was nevertheless sung with supreme skill and know-how.

The first Sinatra/Jobim set comprised a septet of some of the choicest compositions by the celebrated Brazilian, who also played guitar and joined in on the vocal during several titles. Sinatra handled the English lyrics to such jewels as "The Girl From Ipanema", "Meditation", "How Insensitive" and "Quiet Nights Of Quiet Stars" with consummate skill. On standards such as "Change Partners", "I Concentrate On You" and "Baubles, Bangles And Beads" – superbly converted into the bossa nova genre by Frank Sinatra and his newest MD, Claus Ogerma – his phrasing was breathtaking.

Central to the triumphs of *September* and *Sinatra–Jobim* was the singer's unforced depth of expression. On *September*, there was genuine poignancy in his readings of the lyrics, and the series of ten performances he produced for the latter were suffused with a warmth and tenderness which compared favourably with any of his other recordings, no matter what era. As Sinatra himself would say later, he hadn't sung as softly in twenty years.

Two other Sixties albums which were, rightly, given the full promotional treatment were *Sinatra: A Man And His Music* (1965), a two-LP anthology looking back over his career in music and yet another collaboration between musical legends, *Francis A & Edward K. Watertown* (1969) was another matter – a concept album in a basically "contemporary" mould, it was a commercial failure and an artistic success in part only.

The retrospective *A Man And His Music* used recent recordings of pre-Reprise favourites, plus already-released material on that label, along with newly created versions of "I'll Never Smile Again" and "Come Fly With Me". The one-off collaboration with Ellington took place in 1967, *Francis A and Edward K*, didn't quite elicit the kind of magical results so many, including the two leading participants, had hoped for. Sinatra never sings poorly, yet here he didn't sound as inspired as working with Duke Ellington should have occasioned.

The first post-retirement album, *Sinatra & Company*, rescued all but two of the second Sinatra–Jobim get-together. The remaining two tracks, "Bonita" and "Song Of The Sabia", would remain unissued until included in a mid-Seventies British two-LP reissue compilation *Portrait Of Sinatra*. Without equalling the flawless singing on the first LP, there was no doubt that, once

again, Sinatra and his Brazilian friend were completely *en rapport*. "Someone To Light Up My Life" and "This Happy Madness" were the pick of the bunch, together with "Wave", which included what surely must be Frank's lowest-ever note on record: going down with ease to E-flat.

Duke Ellington and Sinatra had a one-off recording date in 1969.

MOVIES

THE DECADE started more or less how the Fifties ended, with two major movies in 1960 – *Can-Can* and *Some Came Running* – and a cameo role in *Pepe*. Over the next 10 years, there were to be further guest appearances in *The Road To Hong Kong* (1962), *The List Of Adrian Messenger* (1963), *The Oscar* (1966) and *Cast A Giant Shadow* (1966).

Sadly, in the Sixties, the non-stop series of films starring Sinatra was largely disappointing. His continued involvement with the Clan (now more often called the Rat Pack) scarcely added to the overall quality of his movies, except for the entertaining *Robin And The 7 Hoods* (1964), a modern day version of the Robin Hood story set in Chicago gangland with a Cahn–Van Heusen score. Otherwise, there were turkeys such as *Sergeants 3* (1962), *4 For Texas* (1964) and *Marriage On The Rocks* (1965). Even these, however, were masterly by comparison with the forgettable, tasteless *Dirty Dingus Magee* (1969).

Background: Robin And The 7 Hoods; Below: The Manchurian Candidate.

Two other less-than-successful Sixties movies were *The Devil At Four O'Clock* (1961) and *None But The Brave* (1965), which marked Sinatra's directorial debut. In *Come Blow Your Horn* (1963), Sinatra again showed a deft comic touch alongside a bevy of glamorous "gals" and, in *The Naked Runner* (1967), Sinatra turned in a good performance as a businessman inveigled into killing a defected British spy.

By far the most important of Sinatra's Sixties films was *The Manchurian Candidate* (1962). Richard Condon's novel, about the brainwashing of a group of captured GIs in Korea, provided Hollywood with subject matter which it had never previously explored so deeply, or so cleverly. Sinatra's Captain Ben Marco is just about perfect, his portrayal both believable and sensitive.

Von Ryan's Express (1965) was one of those entertaining films turned out by Hollywood since the Fifties. Sinatra plays Colonel Joseph L Ryan, the lone Yank among a bunch of British POWs interned at an Italian war camp in 1943. The film's real star, though, was a magnificent old German steam engine.

Assault On A Queen (1966) involved a highly improbable attempt to hijack the liner *Queen Mary* using a reconditioned German U-boat and, in *The Detective* (1968), Sinatra played a dedicated cop. Of the remaining Swinging Sixties productions, there is little to choose between *Tony Rome* (1967) or its companion piece, *Lady In Cement* (1968). Both are taut, well-produced thrillers, with strong supporting casts.

GIGS

The most important performances by Frank Sinatra in the Sixties were the 30 dates he played all over the world in aid of charity between April and June 1962.

There was no symphony-size orchestra this time – after all, Sinatra was paying the costs – but a solid sextet. Whether playing concerts in Mexico City, Tokyo, the Middle East or in Europe (Paris, London, Milan, Rome, Madrid, Athens, Monte Carlo), there was no doubting the overwhelming success of the tour. Not only were prodigious sums of money raised for charity, but the star's performances netted rave reviews everywhere.

Throughout the tour, Sinatra sounded buoyant. Just occasionally, tiredness prevented optimum delivery – as in one of the Tokyo concerts, where a revived "Moon Was Yellow" gave him some trouble, technically speaking. But at the Paris Lido, for example, on June 5, there were no problems [*Sinatra – The Paris Concert 1962*].

Sinatra's two admirable Paris concerts were preceded by four equally successful appearances across the Channel in London. As exhilarating as these performances were, the English capital was going to have to wait a further eight years before welcoming Sinatra back. Once again the Festival Hall was the venue for four charity concerts which illuminated the local music scene on consecutive nights (May 7 and 8) in 1970.

There are many who were present at these concerts who remain convinced that Frank Sinatra can never have sung better at any time during his career. (This writer is one.) As magnificent as his 1962 concerts had been, the two May 1970 concerts were truly something else.

It was the ballads that would really sign, seal and deliver his omnipotence on both evenings. There were nine ballads, first night; 10, the next. Each one was delivered with awesome technical ease and injected with a depth of expression that was astonishing.

Come Fly with Frank! Sinatra charms the citizens of Tokyo during his world charity tour in 1962.

These particular versions of "Autumn Leaves", using the classic Jenkins arrangement, eclipsed even the 1962 interpretation in the same hall. It was the first ballad on both evenings – and almost at once, it seemed, Sinatra had deserted the joyful ambience of the swingers for an atmosphere of near-despair and sadness. This feeling was sustained by what were surely the finest live readings of "Yesterday" by any singer. The most incredible single performance, on both evenings, was "Ol' Man River". Knowledgeable Sinatra connoisseurs remember them as his most technically accomplished interpretations and, just as important, probably the most emotionally charged.

Sinatra returned to the Festival Hall on 16 November to give two further high-calibre performances with an all-British orchestra. Both performances were introduced delightfully by Princess Grace of Monaco.

Concert tours with the big bands of Basie and Rich were also important events in the Sinatra calendar of the Sixties. The decision to take a top-grade outfit on to the road proved to be of signal importance, especially in respect of live appearances outdoors. And the one event which crystallized these kind of future activities was the Newport Jazz Festival gig with Count Basie's orchestra, in July 1965. It indicated to Sinatra that he, too, could replicate what the big-name rock artists and bands were doing at open-air concerts, including oversized festivals like Woodstock and the Isle of Wight.

Both singer and band, conducted by Quincy Jones, were warmly received throughout their one-hour stint at Newport. The wide-ranging programme included "Get Me To The Church On Time", "Fly Me To The Moon", "Street Of Dreams", the crowd-pleasing "Luck Be A Lady", and "I've Got You Under My Skin". "Hello, Dolly" (hardly a jazz-purist choice, despite featuring Harry Edison on trumpet, as on the recording) was the low-point of the 18-number selection.

The major problem, musically speaking, came with the out-and-out ballads. The classic Basie four-in-the-bar rhythm was inappropriate for truly meaningful readings of classics like "In The Wee Small Hours Of The Morning", "It's Easy To Remember" and "Call Me Irresponsible".

By the Forest Hills concert, five days later, this problem was showing signs of being resolved. The Sinatra-Basie partnership grew into compatibility through regular collaboration. With the Buddy Rich Orchestra, by contrast, Sinatra seemed to strike an instant rapport. His five-gig stint with Rich in July 1967 – which opened in Cleveland and ended in Baltimore – found him in far better voice and obviously enjoying the excellent support. There were no rigid 4/4 restrictions with Rich – the swing numbers swung in a gloriously freewheeling way. And the ballads were performed in classic Sinatra style.

In 1971, Sinatra appeared for the farewell concerts in LA. This was not the wise-cracking Sinatra of yore. Obviously moved both by the occasion itself and the responsive presence of an all-star bill

and a star-studded audience, he looked tense and at times close to tears. But ever the true professional, he turned in the kind of performances any self-respecting entertainer would hope for – particularly, it was reported, for the second concert.

He sang songs from every part of his career: "All Or Nothing At All", saluted the all-too-brief period with Harry James ... "I'll Never Smile Again" did the same for the Tommy Dorsey Orchestra. ... "Ol' Man River" took him back to MGM musicals and dozens of Sinatra bravura performances, live and on record ... "Try A Little Tenderness" and "Nancy" were redolent of the Forties; "The Lady Is A Tramp", "Angel Eyes" and "I've Got You Under My Skin" epitomized, in their different moods and ways, the triumphs of post-*Eternity* years ... "Fly Me To The Moon" recalled the happy, swinging years in front of the Basie band ... The personalized statements that were "That's Life" and "My Way" seemed to personify the whole Sinatra aura – songs to which only *he* had truly given meaning .

And it just had to be a genuine saloon song, "Angel Eyes", an enduring jewel in his bulging casket of diverse material, that would take him off stage, at both farewell events ...

Sinatra and Basie – the partnership got better and better.

TELEVISION

SINATRA'S TV activities during the Sixties were dominated by a five-show series under his own name which, at long last, would make him a legend of the small-screen.

Sinatra: A Man And His Music [*Frank Sinatra: A Man And His Music* (1965) on video] was the turning point. With a large orchestra in full view, this includes 17 well-chosen songs – five of which were woven skilfully into a satisfying medley, which was one of several peaks of excellence. And Sinatra is in full control, from the moment he seats himself calmly on a stool for a storming "I've Got You Under My Skin".

It would be difficult for *A Man And His Music, Part 2* – (1966), also on video – to replicate its predecessor's brilliance. Daughter Nancy duets with Dad on "Yes Sir, That's My Baby" and "Downtown". But it was the Ballad Medley which was the single highlight. Using "Just One Of Those Things" as the link song, it was beautifully realized and performed with supreme conviction.

The third in the series was something extra-special. So special, in fact, that *A Man & His Music + Ella + Jobim* – (1967), also on video – will probably never be surpassed. With Riddle wielding the baton, this was as near to being the perfect musical TV show as possible. Sinatra's joy at having Ella Fitzgerald as his principal guest showed in the way he actively encouraged her to perform in the most free-and-easy way – just like a kind of private jam session, instead of a well-structured media presentation. As exhilarating as the Frank-Ella duets were, for many viewers the absolute peak in this remarkable programme was reached when Sinatra, taking vocal lead, and Jobim reproduced in miniature much of the magic of their recordings of "Quiet Nights", "Change Partners", "I Concentrate On You" and "The Girl From Ipanema".

Francis Albert Does His Thing in 1968, the fourth in a series of Sinatra shows.

The fourth show couldn't possibly hope to achieve the artistic heights of the previous year. *Francis Albert Does His Thing* – (1968), also on video – had Don Costa making his Sinatra/TV debut. It also had two guests – Diahann Carroll and the 5th Dimension.

The Ballad Medley in the fifth and last of the series proved to be a major disappointment. This was due to Sinatra suffering from some kind of laryngitic problem. Indeed, it affected practically every number he performed during the simply named *Sinatra* – (1969), also on video.

Surprise! Surprise! *Ol' Blue Eyes is back again . . . !*

Around the time of the White House gig for Richard Nixon and Italian Premier Andreotti, rumours of a Sinatra comeback began to circulate.

Sinatra – mega-star. His insatiable quest to sing before more and bigger audiences would dominate the rest of his career. The Living Legend goes on and on and ...

Towards the end of April 1973, under a heavy cloak of secrecy and in the company of conductor Don Costa, Sinatra entered the Goldwyn Studios in Hollywood armed with two new songs, Kris Kristofferson's "Nobody Wins" and "Noah" by Joe Raposo. These numbers were almost certainly intended for a new LP – unfortunately, it was an unsuccessful session and the masters were destroyed.

Undeterred, Costa and Sinatra – this time joined by Gordon Jenkins – returned to the same studios several times before the end of August. The result was the first comeback album consisting of a dozen numbers by contemporary writers, ranging from Raposo and Kristofferson to Stephen Sondheim and Paul and John Williams.

Its title, *Ol' Blue Eyes Is Back,* gave rise to the most popular Sinatra epithet since "The Voice", and it was also used for the singer's comeback TV special. Transmitted on November 18, 1973, the show offered living proof that he was indeed back, if perhaps a little overweight this time around. But the critics were mostly kind: as the *New York Daily News* put it, "We thought we were through writing love-letters to Frank Sinatra. Here we go again!" If 1973 was the Year Of The Comeback, the rest of the Seventies proved Sinatra was going to be around for a while. 1974 set the pattern with concerts at innumerable venues – from plush indoor night-spots and concert halls to huge outdoor arenas.

It was this insatiable quest to sing before more and bigger audiences that would dominate the rest of Sinatra's career. Unable to exist without adulation, the Living Legend was transforming himself into a modern superstar.

His first full comeback performance took place on January 25, 1974 at Caesar's Palace – his first booking there since 1968. In March, Sinatra embarked on a twelve-concert tour in aid of the Variety Clubs International.

In July, Sinatra returned to Australia on a brief tour that soon ran into problems. True to form, there were several altercations between the visitor and the local press, which included allegations by a cameraman that one of Sinatra's bodyguards had looped an electric flex around his neck. During the rapturously-received 75-minute performance which followed, Frank told the 8,000-strong Melbourne audience what he thought of Australian journalists,

"They are bums and parasites, who have never done an honest day's work. Most of them are a bunch of fags, anyway ..."

adding for good measure that the female variety were

"buck-and-a-half hookers".

As it turned out, this wasn't a smart move. After the Australian Journalists' Association had called upon fellow trades union affiliates to boycott him, Sinatra found there was no one to serve him food and drink, or to carry his baggage; moreover, he couldn't use any form of public transport to get him to the airport ... let alone find anyone to service his private jet.

Following negotiations, apologies came from both sides – as a goodwill gesture, Sinatra took no fee for the third of the Melbourne gigs, *Sydney, July 16, 1974,* which was also televized.

The Seventies were a decade of non-stop touring, at home and abroad.

Back in the US, he appeared in court on charges of ordering his bodyguards to beat up a young insurance agent, Frank

Weinstock, at a Palm Springs hotel. Sinatra's relief at being found not guilty must have been tempered when Jilly Rizzo, his close friend and personal minder, was fined over $100,000 for assault and battery.

Following the case, it was off to Lake Tahoe, Nevada, for seven days at the plush Harrah's in September – and a first-time association with the marvellous Woody Herman band.

After a 24-hour break, the Sinatras quit Tahoe for seven days at Caesar's Palace, and this was followed in October by a nation-wide tour – Woody Herman's splendid young orchestra provided the concerts with their own brand of big-band excitement. And he rounded off a truly energetic year with a memorable performance at the Diplomat, Miami, on New Year's Eve.

1975 saw no let-up in Sinatra's programme. The star played Caesar's Palace on no fewer than four occasions; he visited Europe twice; then, in November, he returned to London, before concerts in Iran and Israel. In all, Sinatra made a remarkable 140 individual performances in 105 days, appearing before audiences in excess of 500,000 at home and abroad.

During his European travels, Sinatra fell out with the German press, arousing much controversy in the process. In London, his rage undiminished, he lambasted German journalists on-stage at the Albert Hall for saying he was "a super-gangster and ... a pathetic alcoholic whose career is over". His torrid outburst went on: "I could have answered them and told reporters to look to the sins of their fathers. I could have mentioned Dachau. They are the gangsters ... "

Within the packed hall, where the audience included Princess Margaret, Princess Anne and Princess Grace of Monaco, a kind of stunned silence prevailed for the most part.

From a personal standpoint, the twelve London concerts of 1975 provided outstanding memories. Sinatra has never disguised his delight at the genuine warmth shown to him on his trips to Britain. Invariably – some might say uncannily – he succeeded in singing at or near to his very best when performing in front of audiences there.

Following the twin triumphs of 1975, his appearances back in London in 1977 and 1978 were, if anything, even more enthusiastically received. And Sinatra himself responded in even finer voice too.

Throughout the Seventies, he shared the stage with a variety of top-grade talent including Ella Fitzgerald, Count Basie, Sarah Vaughan and John Denver. During 1977, Dean Martin and Sinatra worked together for the first time in years and, 12 months

Sarah Vaughan and Frank in rehearsal for their week at the London Palladium with Count Basie in 1975.

on, Sammy Davis Jr also worked briefly with his Rat Pack chief. But by far the most unusual individual gig of the Seventies – geographically speaking – took place on 27 September 1979, when Sinatra performed in Egypt, against a backdrop of the Pyramids. The concert, in aid of a local children's charity, was described by Egyptian President Anwar Sadat as "an unforgettable experience".

The perfect end to the year, perhaps – and indeed the decade – came during his 64th birthday party at Caesar's Palace. Sinatra was visibly moved when presented with the prestigious Pied Piper Award by the American Society of Composers, Authors & Publishers.

For Sinatra, the saddest event of the decade was the death of his mother Dolly. She was travelling from Palm Springs to Las Vegas for the opening night of her son's latest Caesar's Palace engagement, when the Lear jet in which she was a passenger hit a mountain-side. After playing the opening two shows, Frank cancelled the rest of the season. Dolly's death was confirmed, four days later, when her body was recovered from a snow-covered ridge. The funeral took place on 13 January 1977.

Other deaths which caused Sinatra great sadness during the Seventies were those of his mentor Bing Crosby and Hank Sanicola, his former song publisher, plugger and friend. An altogether happier event was his marriage in July 1976 to Barbara Marx, formerly married to Zeppo Marx.

In 1980, he received the Johnny Mercer Award for his "lifetime romance with the American Songwriter" as well as a special Humanitarian Award, for his untiring efforts to raise money for needy and disabled children. From then on, the number of awards, accolades and presentations would continue to increase.

And his singing still made people happy – the 1980 London concerts were a good example. Sinatra appeared, in consecutive week-long stints at the Festival and Albert Halls. At both venues, he performed with undiminished brilliance. And any thoughts that, approaching 65, his appeal must have waned were dispelled by the avalanche of letters requesting tickets.

1981 began with a lengthy application by Sinatra to obtain a licence as public relations and entertainment consultant for his second home – Caesar's Palace. The alleged Sinatra-Mafia link came up again in *The Last Mafioso*, a book based on the confessions of Jimmy "The Weasel" Fratianno, a Mafia hit-man who claimed that Frank had been front-man, acting for Chicago mobsters, in respect of the ownership of a gambling casino at Lake Tahoe, Nevada.

In February, he testified before the Gaming Control Commission, who returned the gaming licence that had been taken away almost 20 years before. President Reagan gave a personal reference, describing Sinatra as "an honourable person".

In July, Frank made his first ever trip to Sun City in *apartheid*-bound South Africa and insisted on playing to non-segregated audiences.

The following January, at Radio City Music Hall, Sinatra and Luciano Pavarotti performed together for the first time. And, once again, Sinatra appeared before a huge audience in the Dominican Republic [*Concert For The Americas,* available on video] accompanied by the Buddy Rich Orchestra. During 1982, he also appeared alongside Nancy Reagan, singing "To Love A Child" on the South Lawn of the White House to promote Mrs Reagan's book about foster-parents.

Within a five-month period in 1983, two of Sinatra's closest and most important musical associates died. Don Costa on 19 January; and Gordon Jenkins on May 1. It was fitting that both these great talents should have contributed significantly to *She Shot Me Down* (1981), the last Sinatra album of genuine quality.

On a happier note, 1983 closed with an all-star party thrown by the Variety Club. Richard Burton delivered a glowing oral tribute. Calling him "a giant", Burton said of Sinatra:

"Other than himself, there is no one who knows the magnitude of his generosity."

Record-wise, 1984 should have provided one album at least that would satisfy both his long-time followers and younger admirers. Even at the age of 68, a Sinatra–Quincy Jones album seemed a perfect way of reviving his recording career. Unfortunately, *LA Is My Lady* (1984) seemed to indicate that, in the area of recording at least, Sinatra should finally close the book.

During the remainder of the Eighties, he continued to strut his stuff on stage but there were worries about his health. In November 1986, surgeons performed an emergency operation to remove an abscess from his large intestine. Two months later, he underwent further surgery. But a third operation, in early February 1987, was less serious – doctors explained it was to remove scar tissue from the previous surgery. Not long after, the redoubtable Sinatra re-commenced gigging.

By June 1988, he had undertaken an Italian concert tour. Three months later, he gave eight performances at Carnegie Hall, with 74-year-old jazz giant Lionel Hampton in support.

In December, at a huge press conference, Sinatra, Dean Martin and Sammy Davis Jr gave the news of an impending 29-city tour, titled "Together Again". The American Express-sponsored tour commenced on March 13 and continued until the 20th, when Martin bowed out.

Sinatra and Davis played a further seven dates in tandem,

before Martin's replacement, Liza Minnelli, made it three again. The new all-star package called itself "The Ultimate Event". For most of 1990, Sinatra's activities would revolve around "The Ultimate Event", with a further tour of the US and Europe. The caravan continued rolling until the middle of the year when an ailing Sammy Davis Jr quit. On May 16, 1990, he died in LA at the age of 64.

In 1990, two further deaths affected Sinatra. In January, he lost long-time friend Harold Arlen, one of the greatest of all pop-music composers. And less than a month later, his very close buddy, songwriter Jimmy Van Heusen, passed on too.

By the end of the year, one thing was certain: it had *not* been a very good year. And there were more grievous losses to come ...

However, neither Sinatra's periods of hospitalization nor the deaths of those close to him could coax the superstar back into retirement – a genuine, no-going-back retirement, this time.

Even so, a growing number of people were beginning to believe – privately and otherwise – that as of now, or very shortly, it really was time for Frank Sinatra to quit. And the reasons were becoming all too obvious, and increasingly so ...

Doin' it their way – Frank and Sammy get their instructions from Liza during one of the hugely successful "Ultimate Events".

1973-1989

RECORDS

In the 11 years following his return to full-time singing, Frank Sinatra cut just half-a-dozen albums: unfortunately, over 60 different recording sessions between April 1973 and June 1988 produced remarkably few items suitable for release.

Ol' Blue Eyes Is Back (1973), however, was as good a comeback album as anyone could have wished for. It featured an intriguing variety of fresh material, including the poignant and unusual "There Used To Be A Ballpark", the celebratory "You Will Be My Music" and, of course, "Send In The Clowns".

The follow-up LP, *Some Nice Things I've Missed* (1974), certainly had its moments, although you couldn't number "Tie A Yellow Ribbon " and Neil Diamond's "Sweet Caroline" among those.

The prospect of a live album with the superb Woody Herman Orchestra in sterling support was mouth-watering. Unfortunately, *The Main Event* (1974) proved to be the first real dud of the post-retirement period. Purported to have been recorded at Madison Square Garden on October 13, the contents were, in fact, pilfered from five different concerts – including Madison Square – between October 2 and 13. It was the kind of dishonesty which record companies have been guilty of for many years but it was still a shame that overall the singing did not match the tremendous support from Herman & Co.

As Sinatra grew older, recordings were all too often aborted and hits grew scarce. In 1974, there was a short-lived chart life in Britain for "I Believe I'm Gonna Love You", which peaked at Number 34, during a low-key, seven-week chart stay.

Six years later, a new Sinatra album was released, a triple-LP set. Titled *Trilogy*, it was conceived in three parts – *Past* (with Billy May arrangements), *Present* (Don Costa, Nelson Riddle) and *Future* (Gordon Jenkins).

Past was the best of the three. Though scarcely vintage Sinatra, it wasn't at all bad. *Present* was less successful. The third part of *Trilogy* is the one which continues to cause the most arguments.

Indeed, it remains the most controversial of any Sinatra record project. Brilliantly written and conceived as it was, there remains an overall aura of sycophancy, combined with pretentiousness, which proved indigestible for many listeners.

Swingin' with Quince – Sinatra acknowledges a long-time musical associate, Quincy Jones.

In fact, by far the best Seventies/Eighties album was *She Shot Me Down* (1981). Its completion at five different dates, over a period of six months, mirrored Sinatra's erratic recording pattern of the time. Material-wise, it was the most intriguing album since, say, *Cycles*. Mostly, it was comprised of new songs, by Jule Styne, with Susan Birkenhead ("Hey Look, No Crying"), Stephen Sondheim ("Good Thing Going"), Pamela Phillips and Don Costa ("Monday Morning Quarterback"), Gordon Jenkins ("I Loved Her"), and Alec Wilder and Loonis McGlohan ("South – To A Warmer Place"). Not all the singing was vintage Sinatra, but he read both the old and the "modern" lyrics with an understanding and technical control that was often lacking in his later recordings.

In his 69th year, Sinatra once again collaborated with Quincy Jones – and he could scarcely have hoped for better sidemen on *LA Is My Lady* . Unfortunately, his voice was not at its best during the three sessions needed to complete the LP. *LA Is My Lady* was released, together with a pedestrian "Until The Real Thing Comes Along", in 1980 – but neither made any impact in any territory worldwide.

Sinatra's recording activities for the decade ended there. (Two special Sinatra collections were released to celebrate his 75th birthday in 1990. Capitol/EMI put together a commemorative three-CD/five-LP box [*The Capitol Years*]. Warner's, not to be outdone, produced its own 81-track, four-CD/six-LP box set –[*The Reprise Collection*]. Both were excellent in concept and production.)

If Sinatra's record output during the later period produced very little substantial product, it did at least create another kind of record when "Theme From New York, New York" became a modest hit in 1980. This meant that Sinatra had equalled the almost unbelievable feat of Louis Armstrong (1926–66) of 40 years in the *Billboard* singles charts. Sinatra's feat had begun with Tommy Dorsey's recording of "Polka Dots And Moonbeams" in 1940 and came full-circle with "New York, New York".

His involvement with recording fading fast, concerts would inevitably come to dominate Sinatra's time in the Eighties.

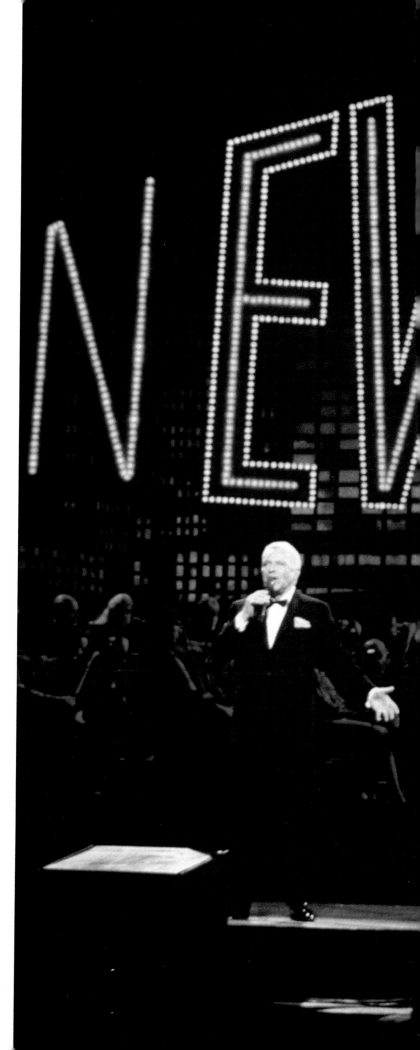

GIGS

The gruelling schedule kept up by Sinatra throughout the Seventies, and for most of the following decade, might have taxed the resources of a man half his age, but he was determined to remain at the top.

After nearly a year of preparation, Sinatra staged his first major comeback performance in January 1974 with his return to Caesar's Palace. Looking fit and healthy, he sang with renewed vigour and much of his pre-retirement magic intact. Even the cancellation of a couple of shows, due to throat problems, couldn't detract from a triumphant return.

On April 8, with Bill Miller conducting, Sinatra made his long-awaited debut at Carnegie Hall, with a well-chosen mix of songs old and new. Soon he was flying off to Japan and Australia: Sinatra took Tokyo by storm, following up his success with a 35-minute show for US service personnel on board the *USS Midway*, moored at the Yokosuka Naval base.

Later that year came eight days at the plush Harrah's, Lake Tahoe, which found Sinatra sharing the spotlight with Frank Jr and Nancy – as well as Woody Herman's "Young Thundering Herd".

The Vegas gigs were a prelude to Sinatra touring with the Herman band for almost a month. Starting in Boston and finishing in Dallas, the itinerary included two outdoor gigs at New York's Madison Square Garden. Although the tour produced much fine music, there were times when the strain of such a punishing schedule showed through and Sinatra sounded tired.

1975 saw further extensive touring. There were superlative performances on two consecutive nights in London (May 29/30) at what the singer had re-titled the "Francis Albert Hall".

On the opening night, Sinatra sang with extraordinary power throughout an 80-minute performance, which included Stevie Wonder's "You Are The Sunshine Of My Life", "My Way", "I See Your Face Before Me', "Last Night When We Were Young", "Cycles", "Strangers In The Night" and, a delightful revival from almost 30 years before, "But Beautiful".

Perhaps the highlight of the year found Sinatra playing two weeks at the famous Uris Theatre in New York in September, joined by Ella Fitzgerald and the Count Basie Orchestra. Ella and Basie took care of the first half. Sinatra, with Basie, closed. At the end of his performance, Frank invited Ella back on stage, for a series of joyous duets.

As the touring wound on relentlessly during the remainder of the Seventies, Sinatra started playing venues he'd almost certainly never worked before (e.g. Tarrytown, New York and the brand new 3,500-seater Westchester Premier Theatre). This unremitting schedule went on into the next decade.

And what better way to start a new decade than by getting your name into the *Guinness Book Of Records*? That's what happened following Frank's first-ever appearance in Rio de Janeiro's vast Maracana Stadium on January 26, 1980. An awesome 175,000 crowd gave him the kind of welcome which, according to one of the musical entourage, "shook us all to the foundations – Frank himself was staggered by the sheer volume of the applause that greeted his arrival on-stage". Sinatra repaid his record audience with an 18-number performance that few of them would ever forget.

Sinatra was equally generous in the size of his programme for his return to Carnegie Hall five months later, where a capacity audience roared its approval at yet another enactment of artistry proving that, in his 65th year, he had taken on a new lease of life.

By September 1984, however, there were tell-tale signs of deterioration in his vocal output during the Albert Hall concerts: the personality of the man was beginning to be of real importance in getting him through the more technically taxing ballads.

Nonetheless, in September 1985, Sinatra appeared in Milan for a lengthy concert appearance that silenced anyone thinking he was over the hill. Forget lack of staying power, the second part of an 80-minute stint turned out better than the first!

"The Ultimate Event" package tours took up a lot of Frank's time during 1988–90. Originally, the idea was for Sinatra, Sammy Davis Jr and Dean Martin to perform under a "Together Again" banner. Each would undertake his own set, with all three stars appearing together for the final section of each concert.

But the Sinatra–Martin–Davis triumvirate lasted only as far as Chicago. On Sinatra's strong advice, it was reported, Martin quit. His performances had been consistently erratic – and some concert-goers had complained that he'd talked more than sung during his contributions.

Sinatra and Davis continued the tour in Cincinnati as a duo, before Liza Minnelli was asked to join them – and the package was retitled "The Ultimate Event". They were to prove a winning team, embarking on a mini world tour in 1988 and continuing intermittently up to late March 1990, when Sammy Davis Jr had to leave.

The personality of the man began to be of real importance in ballads.

TELEVISION

After his comeback in 1973, there were no more TV series in Frank Sinatra's name but he did make numerous guest appearances on other peoples' shows.

The one-off, *Ol' Blue Eyes Is Back* was just the kind of small-screen presentation he needed to advertise his return. Following a sequence of excerpts from his movies, Sinatra and Gene Kelly duetted with charm. The acid test, though, was the classic Ballad Medley. While in no way equalling the superlative medleys from the *Man & His Music* series, quality permeated the readings of "Last Night When We Were Young", "Violets For Your Furs" and "Here's That Rainy Day". All were featured on the video, *Ol' Blue Eyes Is Back*.

The Main Event (1974, available on video) was very much a *live* performance. Taped at Madison Square Garden, *The Main Event* was recorded as part of a tour, which might explain why The Voice was hoarse and rough-edged in places. The ballads, in particular, suffered – "The House I Live In", the penultimate number, came off worst. The audience, though, were over the moon.

Predictably, *Frank Sinatra & Friends* (1977, available on video) proved to be a form of mutual admiration society. After they had contributed one number apiece on their own, friends – like Dean Martin, Tony Bennett and Natalie Cole – engaged Sinatra in duets. More important than these, of course, were Sinatra's own solo efforts, including a hard-swinging "Where Or When", an expressive "Night And Day" and a dull-thud average "Everybody Ought To Be In Love".

Sinatra: The First 40 Years (1980, available on video) was, not surprisingly, cast in a similar mould. Taped at Caesar's Palace on his 64th birthday, the recipient sat in kingly fashion – front row – with wife Barbara and daughters Nancy and Tina in attendance as a bevy of headliners ventured on stage to pay their respects. Naturally, the hero of the hour needed little persuading to take his rightful place on stage to close the evening's proceedings.

Television became less and less important to Sinatra as the Eighties wore on. Perhaps his personal highlight came in 1988 with his two-song salute in *The Tribute To Irving Berlin* show: Sinatra sang "When I Lost You" and "Remember", much to the joy of a crowded Carnegie Hall.

The huge global success of "The Ultimate Event" was also celebrated on video, *Frank, Liza And Sammy: The Ultimate Event*, with contributions from all three participants.

Acting-wise, Sinatra's only small screen appearance of the Eighties came 10 years after *Contract On Cherry* (1977), when the singer played a tough ex-cop in an episode of *Magnum*.

Ol' Blue Eyes is Back – here with his ol' buddy, Gene Kelly – in the TV show of that name.

No One More For The Road

The spirit is willing, but . . . Here's Sinatra, in concert, in Richmond, VA., March 1994, where he collapsed from exhaustion.

At the beginning of December 1994 an announcement was made: following a double-concert at the Fukuoko Dome, Tokyo, later that month, Frank Sinatra would be ceasing live performance forever to concentrate on recording.

Media reaction to this news was curiously muted, perhaps because the decision came as no surprise to those who had been following Sinatra's career.

Years of remorseless touring had taken their toll. Probably the saddest indication of Sinatra's declining powers was the regular presence on-stage of a lyric-prompter, helping the greatest interpreter of the popular lyric to remember his lines even on unforgettable classics such as "They Can't Take That Away From Me" and "My Kind Of Town", songs Sinatra had long since made his own.

Despite being in his seventies, Sinatra kept pushing himself to the limits. In 1990 and 1991, he toured with husband and wife duo Steve Lawrence and Eydie Gorme and played well received concerts in Australia, Norway and Ireland. There was also a brief professional reunion with Shirley MacLaine – but they parted on bad terms.

The following year, Sinatra returned to London, where once again he wowed his audiences. The only major disappointment was the opening night, when the venerable Sinatra showed obvious signs of distraction and provided the author (and others) with first-hand evidence of the debilitating effects of old age: the veteran superstar misread the lyrics of half-a-dozen numbers, as well as re-entering two bars early for an otherwise acceptable "Moonlight In Vermont".

1993 saw no let-up in Sinatra's crowded schedule, which included concerts in Sweden and Germany as well as the usual hectic itinerary in the United States. By this time, however, there had been a sea change in the press's attitude towards the singer. Journalists no longer came to bury Sinatra, but to offer sympathetic praise.

There were particularly joyful reactions to a triumphant five-show stint at the Sands Hotel in Atlantic City in November 1993, as well as the Foxwoods Resort and Casino a year later. However, at Richmond in March 1994, Sinatra collapsed at a Sunday evening concert while singing "My Way".

In the Nineties, all thoughts of a new record were put to one side until the middle of 1993, when Sinatra went back inside the studio at Capitol Tower to lay down his own contributions to a special album project called *Duets*. Thanks to the marvels of modern technology, Sinatra was able to duet with the likes of Barbra Streisand, Tony Bennett, Carly Simon, Charles Aznavour, Aretha Franklin and Bono from U2 without actually being in the same studio at the same time with any of them. Indeed, some of his partners literally phoned their performances in – "digitally" – down the line. Sales in excess of 5 million world-wide guaranteed a *Duets II*, featuring Stevie Wonder and Gladys Knight among others. These albums also inspired a CBS TV special, *Duets*, which arguably overshadowed the Golden Globe-winning mini-TV series, *Sinatra*, reputedly costing $18 million and described as a "candid portrayal" of the singer's life.

Bowing out gracefully after his double triumph in Tokyo in December 1994, Sinatra retired, and never made any more recordings or indeed comeback performances.

Sinatra was last seen in public in January 1996. Rumours of his demise persisted for months before, on May 14th 1998, Ol' Blue Eyes died in Los Angeles from a heart attack at the age of 82. Of all the hyperbole that surrounded Sinatra's life there is one thing we can be certain of: there will never be anyone else like Hoboken's most famous son.

As Sinatra himself declared to the audience at the end of one of his Nineties concerts,

"May you live to 750 and may the last voice you hear be mine..."

Trust Francis Albert to write his own epitaph.

Selected Listings – Records, videos, television and movies

Space considerations preclude full listings. The Discography and Videography, which covers all media, is fairly comprehensive and provides a listing of individual record and video titles, plus sources. Where possible, I have listed CD releases in preference to LPs (which are indicated thus – *). But where important vinyl albums have not been re-released in the compact disc format, LP information is given. Many Sinatra albums can be found – often at favourable cut-down prices – at specialist retail shops or record fairs. The bold numbers ranged right indicate page references in this book.

FRANK SINATRA – THE COLLECTION [1935–54] (3CDs) Hallmark. Sinatra with James, Dorsey, Stordahl, on record, radio.

HARRY JAMES & HIS ORCHESTRA FEATURING FRANK SINATRA: THE COMPLETE COLUMBIA RECORDINGS [1939] Columbia

PORTRAIT OF SINATRA [1939–50] (2CDs) Columbia

TOMMY DORSEY-FRANK SINATRA: "THE SONG IS YOU"
(5 CDs 1940–42) RCA. Boxed set comprising 119 sides which Sinatra recorded with Tommy Dorsey – including 6 alternative takes – together with the quartet of sides he cut with Axel Stordahl while still with Dorsey. In addition, there are 27 tracks of "live" material, the majority of which were unreleased. The latter also includes one of several "farewell-to-the-band" spoken interpolations, involving, not only the leader and his soon-departing vocalist, but also Frank's successor, Dick Haymes. **34, 37**

FRANK SINATRA GREATEST HITS [1940–47] (2CDs) Charly

FRANK SINATRA: THE FORMATIVE YEARS [1942] Avid Records
Comprises seventeen titles with Dorsey and four with James, plus three of the four Sinatra/Stordahl numbers recorded in 1942.

NIGHT & DAY – THE YOUNG SINATRA [1940–44] Conifer

"THAT SENTIMENTAL GENTLEMAN" (2 LPs). [1940, 1942] RCA Victor.
Fascinating collection of Tommy Dorsey airshots (1940–44). Sinatra appears on only five of the titles ("My Melancholy Baby"; "Yearning"; "I'll Take Tallulah"; "Marie"; "The Song Is You").

FRANK SINATRA IN HOLLYWOOD * [1943–49] CBS.
16 commercial recordings of numbers Sinatra sang in Forties movies, including alternative takes of "A Lovely Way To Spend An Evening", "What Makes The Sunset?", "Ever Homeward", plus an unissued version of "The Music Stopped" (3/11/43).

FRANK SINATRA: THE COLUMBIA YEARS: THE COMPLETE RECORDINGS 1943–1952 Columbia. 12 CDs. Boxed set, containing 144-page book which includes complete discography and track-by-track analysis of all known 285 individual numbers. Approx. 150 of these had not been available since original issue; numerous sides (including alternative takes) never previously issued and three tracks ("Nancy"; "Night & Day"; "The

Night We Called It A Day") previously unknown until extensive research was undertaken in 1993. **60**

FRANK SINATRA: THE BEST OF THE COLUMBIA YEARS [1943–52] (4CDs) Columbia. A beautifully put-to-gether cut-down (97 tracks) of the awesome Columbia Years set.

FRANK SINATRA (Previously issued as THE ESSENTIAL FRANK SINATRA 1939–1952) CBS. Boxed set containing insert booklet with in-depth notes by George T Simon. Forty-eight titles, including four numbers featuring Sinatra with James ("From The Bottom Of My Heart"; "Melancholy Mood"; "My Buddy"; "Here Comes The Night").

FRANK SINATRA: THE V-DISCS: THE COLUMBIA YEARS 1943–1952
(2 CDs) Columbia Boxed set, containing complete discographical details of all fifty-three V-Disc recordings, including six hitherto unissued titles. **65**

CHRISTMAS SONGS BY SINATRA [1944–50]

SWING & DANCE WITH FRANK SINATRA [1944–51] Columbia

FRANK SINATRA SINGS HIS GREATEST HITS [1944–52] Columbia

FRANK SINATRA CONDUCTS THE MUSIC OF ALEC WILDER
(Sony). Half-a-dozen sides recorded in 1945, arranged by the composer and conducted by Sinatra, plus excerpts of other Wilder music.

CHRISTMAS SONGS BY SINATRA [1945–47]
Columbia. Ten commercial recordings of Yuletide songs and carols, plus three ex-radio versions of "Ave Maria", "Winter Wonderland", "The Lord's Prayer".

SINATRA SINGS ROGERS & HAMMERSTEIN [1945–51] Columbia

SONGS FOR YOUNG LOVERS/SWING EASY! [1953, 1954] Capitol **18, 86, 88, 91, 102, 105, 120**

HE COMPLETE SINGLES COLLECTION [1953–60] (2CDs) Capitol

FRANK SINATRA/THE COMPLETE CAPITOL SINGLES COLLECTION
(4CDS) [1953–62]

THE CAPITOL YEARS [1953–62] Capitol **148**

IN THE WEE SMALL HOURS [1955] Capitol **19, 91, 105**

HIGH SOCIETY (Original Movie Soundtrack) [1956] Capitol **93, 108, 112**

SONGS FOR SWINGIN' LOVERS [1956] Capitol **18, 91, 104, 105, 120**

CLOSE TO YOU & MORE [1957] Capitol **19, 91, 104, 105**

PAL JOEY (Original Motion Picture Soundtrack) [1957] Capitol **93, 108**

THE SINATRA CHRISTMAS ALBUM [1957] Capitol

A SWINGIN' AFFAIR [1957] Capitol **105, 120**

THIS IS FRANK SINATRA (1953–1957) (2 CDs) Music For Pleasure **102, 105**

(FRANK SINATRA SINGS) ONLY THE LONELY [1958] Capitol **91, 105**

COME FLY WITH ME! [1958] Capitol **91, 105**

WHERE ARE YOU? [1958] Capitol **19, 93, 105**

CAN-CAN (Original Motion Picture Soundtrack) [1959] Capitol **93, 112**

COME DANCE WITH ME! [1959] Capitol

NO ONE CARES [1959] Capitol **19, 93**

THE RARE SINATRA * [1953–59] Capitol

ALL THE WAY [1957–60] Capitol

THE CONNOISSEURS' SINATRA * [1953–60] Capitol

FRANK SINATRA SINGS THE SELECT COLE PORTER [1955–60] Capitol

FRANK SINATRA: THE CAPITOL COLLECTOR'S SERIES
[1953–60] Capitol

NICE 'N' EASY [1960] Capitol **9**

RING-A-DING DING! [1960] Reprise **130**

THE SCREEN SINATRA [1953–60] Music For Pleasure

SINATRA SINGS... OF LOVE AND THINGS * [1957–60] Capitol

Radio Recordings

FRANK SINATRA & JIMMY DURANTE: LEGENDARY SONG STYLISTS

HARRY JAMES & HIS ORCHESTRA: AMERICAN DANCES BROADCASTS * (Jasmine). Two complete broadcasts: the first – featuring two Sinatra numbers ("To You"; "From The Bottom Of My Heart"), linked with the BBC in London.

THE FRANK SINATRA STORY [1935–54] (2CDs) Carlton Double. An historically, as well as musically, – retro of the very earliest Sinatra (*Shine* – Hoboken Four), through various airshots, plus a collection of choice Columbia gems.

TOMMY DORSEY & HIS ORCHESTRA (Jazz Hour) Emanating from the Hollywood Palladium in 1940 and including "The One I Love", "Our Love Affair", "Shadows On The Sand" and "That's How It Goes".

FRANK SINATRA FEATURING TOMMY DORSEY & JO STAFFORD/THIS ONE'S FOR TOMMY 1940–1955 Nine Sinatra/Dorsey airshots, plus Sinatra TV tribute (with Stafford), and rare, one-off reunion between Frank and former boss ('55).

TOMMY DORSEY & HIS ORCHESTRA – LIVE AT THE MEADOWBROOK (Jasmine). Two complete shows – one from the Meadowbrook in 1941 (featuring Sinatra singing "Everything Happens To Me"; "Oh! Look At Me Now"; "Let's Get Away From It All"), and the second from the Capitol, Washington, DC ("Just As I Thought You Were Here"; "You Are Always In My Heart"; "Snootie Little Cutie") — 37

TOMMY DORSEY & HIS ORCHESTRA: 1942 WAR BOND BROADCAST (Jazz Hour). Three Sinatra contributions to this particular war-drive broadcast, plus further Sinatra-Dorsey gems ("Blues In The Night"; "Somebody Loves Me"; "Dig Down Deep") from two other shows.

FRANK SINATRA - ON THE AIR! 1942–1954 (QUE Classics/Tring)

'S WONDERFUL 1943–1954 (CoolNote)

FRANK SINATRA: LIVE 1943–46 (Jazz Hour). Further superior airshots. Most intriguing of all are three numbers ("Couldn't Sleep A Wink"; "Close To You"; "You'll Never Know") with typically gorgeous Stordahl orchestral arrangements which Sinatra would have used at his first (*a cappella*) recording dates for Columbia … But for the AFM strike.

FRANK SINATRA: YOUR HIT PARADE 1944: IT WAS A VERY GOOD YEAR (JRRecords). Skilfully-remastered, 19-number collection of material from some of Sinatra's most important radio series of the Forties, including the complete show of 23/12/44. — 56, 73

FRANK SINATRA: IN CELEBRATION 1944–1955 (Exclusive)

THE OLD GOLD SHOWS/SONGS BY SINATRA 1945–1946 VOLS 1–4 On The Air Double-CD issues of complete SBS shows (two on each CD), plus extra rare Sinatra airshots to make up CD playing time.

FRANK SINATRA: 1946 OLD GOLD SHOWS (Jazz Hour). Two complete Old Gold (January 2 and October 30 1946), with Peggy Lee guest-appearing on the first. Plus a half-dozen fine performances from other shows, including among the six undocumented numbers "What Am I Gonna Do About You?", a Cahn-Styne tune never recorded commercially by Sinatra or anybody else.

THE RAREST SINATRA [1937–46] (Decade Records)

Fascinating collection of broadcast material – including two TV items from 1951 and an absorbing New York-BBC link-up from 1944, with Sinatra singing "These Foolish Things" and "Come Out, Wherever You Are". Earliest item finds a non-singing Sinatra conducting (!) an awful Dixie combo the Four Sharps on Fred Allen's *Town Hall Tonight* show … rare, but understandably so … ?

SINATRA: PORTRAITS FROM THE PAST [1943-46] (Bravura)

Satisfying collection of radio material, a mixture of sings he never did elsewhere, including "I'll Walk Alone", "Three Little Words", "Ac-Cent-Tchu-Ate The Positive".

FRANK SINATRA: "THE VOICE" 1943–1947 (Decade Records).

Yet another fascinating collection of broadcast performances, including two complete shows from December 1943, plus some rare radio-rehearsal material from 1946.

FRANK SINATRA: YOUR HIT PARADE 1947 (JRRecords)

Average-to-good Sinatra fare. **73**

HARRY JAMES & HIS ORCHESTRA: BANDSTAND MEMORIES 1938 TO 1948 (Hindsight). Boxed set, containing 20-page booklet, with performances by several vocalists including Frank Sinatra (seven titles, of which three – "Wishing"; "If I Didn't Care"; "The Lamp Is Low" – he would never record commercially). **32, 37**

FRANK SINATRA: 1949 LITE-UP TIME SHOWS (Jazz Band)

23 performances from Sinatra's last radio series of the Forties-into-the-Fifties, with as varied a mixture as before (e.g. "You're The Cream In My Coffee"; "Body & Soul"; "All Of Me"). **73**

THE UNHEARD FRANK SINATRA, VOLUME THREE: "LONG AGO & FAR AWAY": RADIO RARITIES 1943–1949 (VJC)/**VOLUME FOUR: "I'LL BE SEEING YOU"** (VJC). The most interesting and comprehensive series of Forties material, mostly culled from radio shows and rehearsals of

shows. Vols. I & II are taken from recently-discovered 16" radio discs, in pristine condition. Vol. III is perhaps even more significant: along with radio excerpts, it contains Hollywood Bowl concert material (1945, 1948) of superb quality. **74**

FRANK SINATRA: "THERE'LL BE SOME CHANGES MADE": THE RARITIES 1950–51 (Voice). A 32-number selection of Sinatra's earliest own TV show performances – including duets with June Hutton and Skitch Henderson – which offers conclusive proof that, whatever his personal and professional problems at that time, he still sang with great skill and emotion.

YOUNG FRANK SINATRA: IN THE BLUE OF EVENING (Natasha Imports). 27 tracks featuring a consistently rewarding batch of 1943 War Transcriptions, plus a quartet of Government Transcriptions from 1948, 1952.

SINATRA: THE RADIO YEARS 1939–1955 (Meteor)

The single most comprehensive survey of Sinatra's involvement with radio, including two broadcasts with Harry James, eighteen with Tommy Dorsey and the rest taken from airshots featuring the solo Sinatra, including twenty from the *To Be Perfectly Frank* series. 125 items in all, compiled by the author who also wrote the in-depth booklet and analysis of the contents of this six-CD boxed set. **37, 118**

PERFECTLY FRANK: LIVE BROADCAST PERFORMANCES 1953–1955 (Bravura). A magnificent 31-track selection of the finest singing Sinatra produced on any radio series. Many of the songs (e.g. "You Took Advantage Of Me"; "I'm In The Mood For Love"; "Tenderly") were never recorded commercially by Sinatra. **118**

FRANK SINATRA AFTER HOURS 1953–1955 (Artistry)

LIVE DUETS 1943–1957 (Voice). Duettists included pianist Skitch Henderson (medley of nine tunes), Dinah Shore, Dorothy Kirsten, Nat Cole, Margaret Whiting – all from radio; and Bing Crosby, Louis Armstrong – from TV shows. **73**

* GOT THE WORLD ON A STRING (Starburst)

Twenty superb examples of Sinatra's finest radio series (*To Be Perfectly Frank*), including "Thou Swell", "Just You Just Me", "Where Or When", "Platinum Blues". **97**

Recordings of Gigs

FRANK SINATRA LIVE, VOLUME 4 (Golden Age)

Rumoured at one time to have been taped by Capitol for release as Sinatra's first live album, this splendid eighteen-song performance was recorded in Seattle, Washington, in June 1957. Nelson Riddle conducts as Frank reprises classics such as "You Make Me Feel So Young", "The Lady Is A Tramp"' "My Funny Valentine"' "One For My Baby"… and sings his latest single, "Hey! Jealous Lover", under protest… !

SINATRA: BLACKPOOL, 1953 (JR Records)

FRANK SINATRA: MONTE CARLO 1958 (JRRecords)

Complete concert, introduced inimitably by Noel Coward, before the Monaco Royal Family, plus other distinguished guests. Customary Sinatra fare – including "I've Got You Under My Skin", "April In Paris", "I Get A Kick Out Of You" and "You Make Me Feel So Young" (a request-encore for

Princess Grace), plus an uninhibited "Road To Mandalay" **119–121**

FRANK SINATRA WITH THE RED NORVO QUINTET, 1959 (Blue Note)

THE SINATRA SAGA (Bravura)

Thirty-nine live performances, encompassing the Fifties-through-the-Eighties and including excerpts from a 1959 Australian concert with the Red Norvo Quintet and a trio of numbers with the Basie Band in the Sixties. All in all the Voice doesn't sound too bad. **121**

DECEMBER DOWN UNDER, 1961 (Masterworks)

SALOON SINGER (Encore Records).

Two-thirds of the never-released Reprise-cut Live-at-the-Sands session in November 1961 (including "Moonlight In Vermont"; "Here's That Rainy Day"; "In The Still Of The Night"; "Please Be Kind"), plus all his solo items (*sans* Martin, Davis) at the Villa Venice, Chicago, gig of December 1962.

SINATRA: LONDON ROYAL FESTIVAL HALL, JUNE 1, 1962 (JR Records, 2CDs)

FRANK SINATRA & SEXTET LIVE IN PARIS [1962] Reprise

Sixteen individual performances in all.

SINATRA: THE PARIS CONCERT/RECORDED LIVE

AT THE LIDO, JUNE 5, 1962 (Encore).

The title says it all – one of the world charity tour concerts, with Sinatra in sparkling form throughout this 23-number concert. Bill Miller leads a spirited sextet from the piano. "Moonlight In Vermont", "Night & Day", and, yes, both 'April in Paris' and "I Love Paris" feature among the titles. **137**

THE FRANK SINATRA SPECTACULAR, 1965 (Shine Box) With Basie, Martin, Davis.

FRANK SINATRA: A MAN & HIS MUSIC (Golden Age)

Two separate programmes – and consistently fine singing at a concert from November 1965 – forms the major part of this CD. The rest comprises short, one-chorus versions of a dozen Sinatra favourites, recorded in Italy during the world tour for a commercial project involving local TV.

THE HISTORIC OAKLAND COLISEUM CONCERT, MAY 22, 1968

(BaySound)

SINATRA: THE LOST LONDON CONCERT, 1970

FRANK SINATRA: WASHINGTON, DC, 1973 (JRRecords). Sinatra at the White House – and introduced by "Tricky Dicky" himself – just prior to the re-emergence of Ol' Blue Eyes. Easing his way back into the limelight, with the likes of "One For My Baby", "I Have Dreamed", "Try A Little Tenderness" and, of course, patriotic-plus on "The House I Live In".– just ten numbers in all. **140**

SINATRA: SYDNEY, JULY 16, 1974 (JR Records)

FRACIS (ROYAL) ALBERT HALL, 1975 (Melcone)

SINATRA IN THE SPOTLIGHT * (Retrospect, 2 LPs)

With orchestra conducted by Don Costa, Sinatra sounds inspired by the enthusiastic response from a packed Montreal Auditorium in May 1975. Repertoire includes revived oldies, "But Beautiful", "This Love Of Mine" and "Put Your Dreams Away", the usual regulars, plus the Jenkins-arranged, Legrand-composed "Saddest Thing Of All", recorded the previous fall.

FOR THE GOOD TIMES (Boardwalk)

Extracts from Sinatra gigs at Resorts International, Atlantic City, 1979.

THE SINATRA SAGA, VOLUME 2 (Bravura)

Twenty more live tracks from 1976 to 1986. The voice tends to sound a tad more roughed-up on the later performances (e.g. "Here's To The Band", "Change Partners"). Overall sound, like its predecessors, is good. **121**

THE HOMECOMING CONCERT, 1986 (Orchid)

SINATRA 80th: LIVE IN CONCERT (Capitol)

A SWINGIN' SUMMIT (Pinnacle) Principally, Ella's Concert with Basie, plus Special Guest Frank Sinatra.

FRANK SINATRA – LIVE IN ITALY (Disc Magic)

A well-produced, triple-pack CD set celebrating three separate visits to Italy. The first – and best – finds him accompanied by the Bill Miller Sextet during his 1962 charity world tour; Disc Two has Miller directing the John Flanagan Orchestra, twenty-four years later; the third has Sinatra with Ultimate Event compadres, Minnelli and Davis, in 1989, and, like the other two, was recorded in Milan. Two bonus tracks, including the "High Hopes" promo disc for JFK ... plus a personal "We Thank You, Frank" vocal tribute by International Sinatra Society President, Gary Doctor ...

TV

FRANK SINATRA: "THERE'LL BE SOME CHANGES MADE": THE RARITIES

[1950–51] (Voice)

THE EDSEL SHOW (Loota)

The legendary CBS/TV special of October 13 1957, hosted by Crosby and co-starring Louis Armstrong and Rosemary Clooney. Bob Hope makes a surprise cameo appearance during the "World Tour" medley. The Sinatra-Armstrong "Birth Of The Blues" is, in Sinatra parlance, a "gasser". **117**

WE'D LOVE TO HAVE YOU * (Castagna)

A brace of late-Fifties Sinatra TV shows – featuring the McGuire Sisters (15/11/57) and Eddie Fisher (28/3/58) respectively. Great Sinatra singing on both:

on the first, "Three Coins In The Fountain", "Baby, Won't You Please Come Home?", on the second: "Taking A Chance On Love", "Time After Time"

WE'VE GOT THE NUMBERS OTHERS DREAM ABOUT! * (Castagna).

Two more Sinatra TV shows – the first with Van Johnson as special guest (28/2/58); the second with Edie Adams and Stan Freberg (7/3/58). Frank scores with "Come Fly With Me", "There's No You"; then, with an electrifying "I'm Gonna Live Till I Die" and a touching "One For My Baby" on the latter show.

"SINATRA": MUSIC FROM THE CBS MINI-SERIES [1994]

(Warners, 2 CDs). Twenty-six original Sinatra recordings – one with Harry James, six with Tommy Dorsey, plus material from Columbia, Capitol and Reprise (1944–79). Also included are tracks by Crosby (2), Benny Goodman, Billie Holiday. **153**

Movies

TWO ORIGINAL MOTION PICTURE SOUNDTRACKS: "SHIP AHOY!

"/"LAS VEGAS NIGHTS" * [1942/1941] (Hollywood Soundstage) **35**

ORIGINAL MOTION PICTURE SOUNDTRACK:

"HIGHER & HIGHER" * [1943] (Hollywood Soundstage) **56, 65**

"HIGHER & HIGHER" [1943] & **"STEP LIVELY"** [1944] (Grant Movie Themes)

ORIGINAL SOUNDTRACK RECORDING: "ANCHORS AWEIGH!" *

[1945] (Curtain Calls) **56, 69, 76**

FROM THE ORIGINAL SOUNDTRACK – "TILL THE CLOUDS ROLL BY"

[1946] (Sandy Hook) **69**

"ON THE TOWN": ORIGINAL SOUNDTRACK

[1949] (Show Biz Records) **70**

"ON THE TOWN" [1949] /"ANCHORS AWEIGH!"** [1945] (Blue Moon)

THE SOUNDTRACK SESSIONS (Bravura)

A marvellous collection of Sinatra' movie items. All nine songs from the soundtrack of *Meet Danny Wilson* (including an alternative take of "I've Got A Crush On You"), supported by his exhilarating vocal contributions to the never-completed *Finian's Rainbow* animation project (including duets with Ella and Louis Armstrong). If all that isn't enough, there are the vocals from *The Joker Is Wild*, plus "If I Loved You" (from *Carousel*, the movie from which Frank walked), the

unreleased title tune from *The Man With The Golden Arm* and the song Sinatra recorded specially for *Advise & Consent*. **108**

FRANK SINATRA: "THERE'LL BE SOME CHANGES MADE": THE RARITIES [1950–51] (Voice)

"GUYS & DOLLS" [1955] (M.P.T.1)

ROBIN & THE 7 HOODS ∗ (Original Motion Picture Soundtrack) [1964] Warner Brothers **136**

Video

Movies

TV:

Movies

Step Lively – but that's the last thing on Frank's mind.

BIBLIOGRAPHY

Sinatra! The Song is You, Will Friedland

All or Nothing at All: A Life of Frank Sinatra, Donald Clarke

Sinatra: His Life and Times, Fred Dellar

An American Legend, Nancy Sinatra

Sinatra: An American Classic, John Rockwell

The Great American Popular Singers, Henry Pleasants

Sinatra, Robin Douglas Home

The Voice: The Story of An American Phenomenon, EJ Kahn, Jr

Frank Sinatra: A celebration, Derek Jewell

The Films of Frank Sinatra, Gene Ringgold, Clifford Mc Carty

Frank Sinatra at the Movies, Roy Pickard

Sinatra, Earl Wilson

Sinatra and the Great Song Stylists, Ken Barnes

Sinatra, The Man and His Music, Ed O'Brien, Scott P, Sayers Jr

The Sinatra File, Part Two (second edition), John Ridgway

Index

Picture Credits

The publishers would like to thank the following sources for their kind permission to reproduce the photographs in this book:

Hulton Deutsch Collection 56, 120/1, 137, 138; **London Features International** 4(top right), 4(top centre right), 4(bottom centre right), 9, 11, 16, 25, 30, 33, 38, 39, 40, 42, 46, 57, 60, 61, 65, 67, 70, 81, 85, 87, 88, 90, 96, 103, 106, 108, 112, 116, 117, 127, 132(bottom left), 136, 141(bottom), 141, 147, 151, 157; **Pictorial Press** 4(bottom centre), 10, 26, 27, 28/9, 35, 52, 53, 54, 55, 62, 66, 68, 69, 71, 72, 73, 76, 82, 89, 92/3, 95, 99, 100, 101, 104, 107, 109, 113, 115, 122/3, 125, 126, 131, 135, 136, 155; **Range Bettmann UPI** 4(top right), 4(top centre), 4(centre middle top), 4(bottom left), 4(bottom centre left), 4(top centre left), 4(centre middle bottom), 6/7, 13, 14/5, 16, 19, 20, 22, 36, 41, 43, 44, 45, 48, 49, 50, 51, 58, 63, 64, 69, 75, 78/9, 79, 80, 84, 97, 98, 110, 111, 119, 128, 132/3, 138, 139, 140, 142, 143, 159; **Rex Features** 153, Dezo Hoffmann 132, 156, Nils Jorgensen 145, LGI 148/9, Yoram Kahana 150, SIPA 18, 21, Richard Young 3.